ALASDAIR HUTTON ... ... yal
Edinburgh M ... ... itten and
introduced hundreds of events and concerts in Scotland and
around the world. As well as writing the history of the 15th
Scottish Vol... ... ... of the B... ... ...

Ireland and was Mem...
Convener of Scottish B... ... ...ie lives in the Scottish Borders tow... ... ...

FRONT COVER TARTAN RIBBON is The Royal Edinburgh Military Tattoo Tartan
(Scottish Register of Tartans reference STA2614) based on a Wilsons of Bannockburn
sett, designed by Peter MacDonald in 1998 for the Edinburgh Military Tattoo to
celebrate their 50th anniversary in 2000. The colours depict the three military
forces – Navy, Army & Air Force with the black from Edinburgh's heraldic arms.

By the same author:

The Tattoo Fox, Luath Press 2013
The Tattoo Fox Makes New Friends, Luath Press 2014

The Greatest Show on Earth

Behind the Microphone at The Royal Edinburgh Military Tattoo

ALASDAIR HUTTON

with a Foreword by Brigadier David Allfrey

Luath Press Limited

EDINBURGH

www.luath.co.uk

First published 2016

ISBN: 978-1-910745-69-4 paperback
ISBN: 978-1-910745-80-9 hardback

The paper used in this book is recyclable. It is made
from low chlorine pulps produced in a low energy,
low emission manner from renewable forests.

Printed and bound by Martins the Printers Ltd, Berwick upon Tweed

Typeset in 10 point Sabon by Main Point Books, Edinburgh

Contents

This book is dedicated to the thousands of performers from around the world who have given me so much pleasure and to the many talented people in The Royal Edinburgh Military Tattoo team and the other tattoos and shows who have been kind enough to ask me to join them and have been such good friends.

Acknowledgements

I HAVE RECEIVED tremendous help from the staff
of the Tattoo office in verifying information and
digging out pictures to illustrate the text. In particular
Rachel David went beyond the call of duty.

Shona McMillan took the splendid photographs behind the
scenes on pages 1, 31, 34, 217 and on the back cover.

The pictures on pages 19 and 21 are from the
archives of the Royal Military School of Music.

Several friends have reminded me of details which
had slipped through the sieve of my memory.

Foreword

SINCE EARLIEST TIMES history, legends and ideas have been passed from generation to generation through the spoken word, in poetry, in songs, in music and in written form.

Everyone loves a good story and we are all enthralled by those who can tell them, particularly when a tale is delivered using rich language and with passion. In many theatrical productions, as with the ancients, the storyline can be held by a third party observer or a narrator. So it is with The Royal Edinburgh Military Tattoo.

For the last 25 years, Alasdair Hutton has told our story to each of our audiences since he started in 1992 – a total live audience of over five million people. Not only has he been behind the microphone without fail, in Edinburgh and when we have taken the show abroad, but he has also researched and written the script: not just the core story but also a vast store of 'reserve' passages that can be called on to cover some mishap or cope with the unexpected. Accordingly, Alasdair not only represents the Tattoo's corporate memory but he is the font of our knowledge. He knows each of the acts, the personalities involved and their music and he can answer just about any question you care to ask about our nation's history and the parts played by the Armed Forces. His memory is phenomenal and I have never seen him caught out. Even with last-minute changes in the VIP plot and an unexpected guest getting out of a car, he can conjure up the right and proper words of welcome. He does this with consummate calm, an easy professionalism and good grace. This is a special talent.

Each evening starts with Alasdair's 'journey around the world'. He takes to the microphone and personally invites the audience to join him for the evening, singling out each region of the world in turn, asking everyone to cheer in recognition of their own place. When I took over as Producer in 2011, I felt this practice might be a little outdated, a little cheesy. I discussed with Alasdair what we might do instead. But, as I listened night after night, I realised that it was this device which acted as the catalyst for an atmosphere that offered every member of our audience a real sense of belonging for the 90 minutes of our show. His words did not simply welcome everyone to Scotland, to Edinburgh, to the Castle and to the Tattoo – each person was being invited to attend, on their own terms and proud of their own identity, irrespective of what that might be, and to come together for a special evening of entertainment and inspiration.

Alasdair's most precious talents are his voice, his sense of timing and his feel for occasion. He understands instinctively what is needed for any moment in the show, whether it be a single word to act as a signpost or a longer narrative to set the scene. His voice is 'caramel', carrying just enough gentle brogue to hold audiences' desire for a Scottish flavour but also not so much that words or meaning might be lost. For many of our audience, English is not their first language and yet, many are able to follow the story, as much through Alasdair's inflections as anything else.

For The Royal Edinburgh Military Tattoo, the music and sound lie at the heart of the performance. Every note is carefully captured through multiple microphones and engineered through complex software and the mixing desks to deliver a stunning orchestration to every one of our 8,800 audience members. The performers move, of course, sound bounces off the Castle walls and the stands and it travels differently every night depending on the weather and the crowd – physics is horrid. Despite all this, the storyteller must deliver his words flawlessly every time, without a stumble or a tic and without always hearing them coming back accurately. He must train himself to ignore extraneous sounds, echoes and a producer asking silly questions at key moments! The storyteller is uniquely exposed. He is on his own and any slip is detected instantly by everyone. The role demands skill and lots of nerve.

My foreword so far has suggested the scale of Alasdair's intellect and his skill. But, I reserve my greatest accolade for his character. Alasdair Hutton is above all one of life's great gentlemen. Not only is he impeccably polite but he has great charisma, values and a wonderful sense of purpose. Each evening he will not just give of his best, irrespective of how he might be feeling, but he will pursue excellence as if there is always some higher standard to be attained. Every night, his script is dotted with amendments as he fine tunes his story and its delivery.

He is also my friend! I have hugely enjoyed our meetings as we develop the show each year and one of my greatest pleasures is meeting him for tea somewhere in Edinburgh – or some further flung place – to tune his final script and ensure it leads the production just so. Alasdair's words are the banister-rail onto which everyone holds as each night's performance moves forward. My greatest fear is that one night he might feel unwell or unable to be there and I might have to step up to his microphone and be horribly exposed!

This book, which is Alasdair's own story – only a small part of it! – gives a sense of the huge contribution he has made to the remarkable institution of The Royal Edinburgh Military Tattoo. He has been the narrator for more than a third of our six decades and has added immeasurable value and colour over that time. He has ensured that Sir Walter Scott's words are recognised around the world and he epitomises the central notion that lies behind the success of the Tattoo: 'Arrive as Strangers – Leave as Friends'. He is *the* storyteller.

Brigadier David Allfrey MBE
Chief Executive and
Producer, The Royal
Edinburgh Military Tattoo

Introduction

I HAVE HAD the rare joy of being lucky enough to narrate The Edinburgh Military Tattoo, The Royal Edinburgh Military Tattoo since 2010, for 25 years so I thought I would take a look over my shoulder at the many tattoos which have given me so much pleasure over those years.

This is merely my own view of the tattoos with which I have been involved, many other people will have seen them differently. I did not keep a detailed diary so many of the things I have recalled are drawn from my memory which may be flawed, although my old scripts have helped to blow the dust off many recollections. I have been lucky enough to work with a host of really talented and fascinating people and have tried to mention as many of them as I could – and I apologise if I have inadvertently missed anyone I ought to have mentioned.

From the start I was fortunate to be asked to write and narrate many other tattoos, as well as concerts and other military events, at home and abroad. I have added notes about some of these as well.

I am solely responsible for the material in this book so all the mistakes are mine alone.

Of course when you are part of an event as big as Edinburgh or even just a small local one, the audiences are vital. Without them there is no point in doing the show and without them the pleasure would be only a fraction of what it is when you hear an excited crowd going home having thoroughly enjoyed themselves and knowing you have helped in that just a little.

Alasdair Hutton
Kelso, 2016

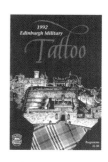

The programme of my first Tattoo in 1992.

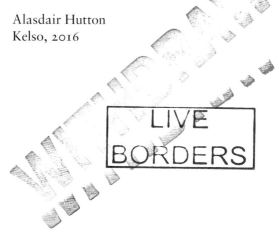

A Brief History of Tattoos

TATTOOS HAVE A long history as military entertainments stretching back to 1742 when they first made their appearance under the name of tattoo. Before that, 'tattoo' was a military necessity, the Army's way of shouting 'time, gentlemen, please' to the soldiers of the Duke of Marlborough's army in their winter quarters in the Netherlands in the late 17th and early 18th centuries.

In the 21st century they have become really popular events. Large or small, tattoos always seem to attract good audiences. Maybe it is because of the spectacle of marching bands in colourful uniforms, maybe it is because of the quality and type of music they play, maybe it is because of the sheer variety of performers which most tattoos are able to muster and sometimes, as in the case of Edinburgh, it is the spectacular setting.

In the 18th century, as now, soldiers would go out to the pubs at night. The Army imposed a curfew which was beaten by drummers at 9.30pm. In those days drums were still the way orders were passed, particularly across the noise of battle.

That 'drink up and go home' signal was known in Dutch as 'Doe den taptoe' or in English 'Turn off the taps'. A soldier then had 30 minutes to get back to wherever he was sleeping before lights and fires were extinguished and the night routine began.

Because 'taptoe' is pronounced 'taptoo' in Dutch it soon became corrupted to 'tattoo' and its spelling in English is its only resemblance to the name for the South Pacific body markings which also seem to be popular with soldiers and other people world-wide.

Armies have an ingrained habit of holding on to practices long after they have been overtaken by time. But they do not cling on to outdated ways of doing things – they simply adapt them to a new use. Then people quickly forget why the old use was ever there in the first place and grow fond of the new one.

There are good examples of that in other military practices today. For example Beating Retreat started as a medieval practice of calling in troops at the end of a day's fighting and is now a good excuse for a cocktail party with musical entertainment. Trooping the Colour was once a practical way to show all troops their special colour or flag to which they should rally in the noise and smoke of battle if they became detached from their comrades. Colours were last carried into battle in 1881 but today they are trooped annually by the Household troops on the Sovereign's birthday or whenever a unit receives a new set of colours.

And so it was with tattoo. When barracks began to be built and it was no longer necessary to beat tattoo to chase soldiers out of the pubs, the practice simply turned into an entertainment. In the 19th century it became an impressive torchlight parade which steadily grew in popularity into the big tattoos of the 20th and 21st centuries.

These early shows also took in the tradition of including a hymn towards the end of the ceremony which had come from Imperial Russia where the Czarist soldiers, who were conscripted virtually for life from the pious peasantry of the country, developed the practice of singing a chorale each night after tattoo to give thanks for having survived another day, and their tradition spread first to the Catholic Army of Austria and then to the Lutheran Army of Prussia and so to other countries in Europe.

The great rise of tattoos as a huge popular spectacle in Britain late in the 19th century originated from a special display arranged for Queen Victoria in 1894. The Queen's third son, the Duke of Connaught who commanded the Aldershot garrison, arranged a drill display in the afternoon which was followed in the evening by bands playing, with soldiers carrying flaming torches interspersed between their ranks for the Queen's entertainment during one of her visits to the Royal Pavilion.

Such torchlight tattoos later became a feature of the

Military Fete which started at Government House in Farnborough in 1900 and included military displays and fairground rides. The last feature of these fetes was a musical display, with the bandsmen accompanied by torch-bearers. On the last note of the 'last post' the flames were extinguished, plunging the whole area into darkness.

After the Great War, the events turned to using searchlights instead of burning torches and these searchlight tattoos took place on a number of evenings during Ascot week in June. Gangs of unemployed men were given work levelling the Rushmoor Arena in Aldershot, which became the home of the tattoo.

These tattoos consisted of massed bands, drill displays, fireworks, lantern displays and theatrical exercises of modern warfare all illuminated by searchlights.

The first historical display took place in 1925, with a recreation of the burning of Moscow, accompanied by the '1812' overture, and later there was a re-creation of the Battle of Waterloo.

These tattoos were nationally renowned, with

The Massed Bands at a rehearsal for the 1914 Aldershot Tattoo.

crowds of up to half a million people attending each year from all over the country. Special transport was chartered, His Master's Voice (HMV) produced recordings of the event and the performances were broadcast on the wireless to Britain and other European countries. The tattoo was so popular that local people came out to watch the huge numbers of cars travelling to Aldershot and in 1930 it took until 6.00am the following morning to clear the queue of cars leaving the area.

With around 5,000 soldiers taking part and over 1,000 soldiers involved in the administration, organising the tattoos was no easy task.

Soon after each tattoo finished, work began on the following year's programme with historical direction in the hands of a military historian on the Reserve of Officers. Historical accuracy during the re-enactments was so important that when the tattoo was to feature the Battle of Waterloo, two French Officers were brought over to ensure that the French uniforms and weapons were recreated properly.

Attention to detail did not stop with historical accuracy, each set or prop was built to look realistic. Chariots and carriages were made up on General Service wagons in the Field Stores workshops which also made spears, ballistas, dummy guns and a host of other props. Sometimes items were even purchased from film companies, bayonets were made with rubber ends in order to prevent injuries during charges, which the organisers wanted to look as real as possible. Elaborate sets were built – including mock Tudor castles, forts and French villages – using the skills of a local company.

The pageants depicted in the Aldershot Tattoo in the 1920s and '30s covered many centuries of history including the Crusades, the Romans in Britain, the Battle of Hastings, the Battle of Agincourt, the Field of the Cloth of Gold, Queen Elizabeth's Visit to Tilbury, the Legend of Drake's Drum, the Siege of Namur, the Battle of Dettingen, the Passage of the Douro, the Retreat to Corunna, the Duchess of Richmond's Ball before Waterloo, the Battle of Inkerman, Gordon and the Sudan and right up to the Great War.

The searchlights which illuminated these shows were the responsibility of the Corps of Royal Engineers. In 1939, at what was to be the last of these Aldershot Tattoos, 33 searchlights were used, producing three billion candlepower of lighting. Those searchlights were not cheap, costing around £5,000 each even then.

Keeping the thousands of troops marching in time gave full rein to the Army's ingenuity. They used lights which flashed in time with the music to keep the soldiers and bandsmen in step. There were also traffic lights behind the scenes telling the soldiers when they were to go on 'stage'. Red lights told them to stop, green to go, and amber to pause. In the 1930s during rehearsals photographs were taken at one second intervals to allow the commander in charge to see if any soldiers were out of step and to reprimand the culprits!

As the years went by, the organisation of the event became enormously complicated. The Royal Automobile Club put up signs 20 miles away directing the huge volume of traffic and special trains were run to handle the numbers of people who wanted to attend.

It became a grand social event as well and members of the Royal Family would attend. When the Royal Princesses Elizabeth and Margaret came in 1935 they were treated to an impromptu fireworks display when a truck laden with fireworks and explosives caught fire. It wowed the children who were arriving for the rehearsal and thought it was all part of the show.

But Hitler and his Nazis put a stop to all that and the Aldershot Tattoo in June 1939 was to be the last before the outbreak of war. A version of the 'Changing of the Guard' symbolically portrayed the move to the khaki-clad mechanised force which was replacing the colour and spectacle that had been so much a part of the public's view of the British Army for centuries.

The Old and New Guards slow-marched forward in turn to present arms, while a light tank moved into position in the centre of the arena. The Commanding Officer of the Old Guard handed over the Union Jack flag to his opposite number who placed it on the tank and, with the growing expectation of war, the massed bands marched off at the end of the Tattoo playing 'Who's Afraid of the Big Bad Wolf?'

After the Second World War, in spite of various attempts to revive it, Aldershot could never recover those golden years. Other places had held tattoos – Cardiff, Colchester, Tidworth, Wembley and Woolwich among them – but by a quirk of fate and the talent of the early producers Scotland has become the world's greatest exponent of tattoos and as anyone in the capital knows, the world beats a path to Edinburgh every summer to watch the greatest show of its kind anywhere on earth.

But it was no accident that Edinburgh put on this great show.

The pipers and drummers of the Royal Irish Fusiliers in front of the elaborate scenery at the 1937 Aldershot Tattoo.

Why Edinburgh?

IMMEDIATELY AFTER THE Second World War there was a great movement to lift the spirits of the British people.

Rudolf Bing, knighted for his services to the arts in 1971, was a member of an Austrian Jewish family who had left Vienna for the United Kingdom in 1934 to escape the rising anti-Semitism of the Nazis in his country. When he became a naturalised British citizen in 1946 he was already canvassing support for the creation of an arts festival which would achieve an international reputation in Britain.

Sir Rudolf was an opera impresario who had helped to found the Glyndebourne Festival Opera and he floated his idea of a rather larger arts festival to the cities of Oxford and Cambridge which both turned down the idea.

Then in 1946 he was introduced to the Lord Provost of the City of Edinburgh, Sir John Falconer, by Harvey Wood who represented the British Council in the city. The Lord Provost was a son of the manse and a lawyer who had fought with the Royal Scots in the First World War. He joined Edinburgh Town Council in 1932 and was elected the City's Treasurer in 1940.

Sir John had been elected Lord Provost in 1944 and when he met Rudolf Bing he quickly saw the economic potential of the Festival for his city in the austerity of the post-war years. Under his drive the Corporation of the City of Edinburgh grasped the nettle that the other cities had refused and on 26 September 1946 voted the money for an International Festival of Music and Drama. With this civic encouragement more money came from the Earl of Rosebery and the British Council.

Determined people make things happen and less than a

year later the new Festival was born, following a service in St Giles Cathedral, with a concert at the Usher Hall at 7.30pm on Sunday 24 August 1947 when Paul Paray conducted the Colonne Concerts Orchestra with members of the Royal Family in attendance.

With preparations for this first Festival under way, Lord Provost Falconer was not a man to let the grass grow under his feet and as an old soldier as well as the civic head he went to talk to General Sir Philip Christison, the General Officer Commanding the Army in Scotland.

Sir Philip had won fame at the Battle of Loos in 1915 as a young officer in the Queen's Own Cameron Highlanders when he leaped from his trench to rally a group of Camerons by singing in Gaelic the stirring 'March of the Cameron Men', and he readily accepted this unusual request for the Army to add its contribution to the new festival with a display of piping

Edinburgh Castle provides the most magnificent setting for the Tattoo.

and dancing on the Esplanade of Edinburgh Castle.

As a start it was rather primitive compared with today's massive organisation, with a few rows of chairs and benches around the Castle Esplanade for spectators to watch the pipers and dancers.

Roddy Martine, in his 2001 history of the Tattoo, quotes the former City Chamberlain, Dr Cecil Stout, as recalling 'going to the Esplanade one wet evening to find the Queen of the Netherlands sitting on a chair with her umbrella up cheerfully enjoying the performance.'

In 1948, the first Olympic year after the War when the Games were held in war-ravaged London, there was military music during August on alternate evenings up on the Esplanade and down in Princes Street Gardens with displays of drill and Highland dancing.

The following year 2,500 people stood around the Esplanade for a popular and successful display entitled *The King's Men* which included music from the bands of the Royal Scots and the Highland Light Infantry and the ceremony of Changing the Guard by the Scots Guards and the 9th Lancers.

That had followed another successful show in the Ross Bandstand in Princes Street Gardens under the title of *Something about a Soldier* which had borrowed its title from the popular song sung by Cicely Courtneidge in the film *Soldiers of the King.*

That show also had music played by the Royal Scots and the Highland Light Infantry and community singing. As Roddy Martine recalls, the people in the crowd were visibly moved when they were asked to sing 'Keep Right on to the End of the Road' to remember its writer Sir Harry Lauder, who was lying gravely ill at his home in Strathaven and who died early the following year.

Both of those performances were produced by Lieutenant Colonel George Malcolm of Poltalloch, so when Sir John Falconer's successor as Lord Provost of Edinburgh, approached the General Officer Commanding the Army in Scotland with a proposal that the Army should present an annual military show to be called the Edinburgh Tattoo, he was the obvious choice to take

THE GREATEST SHOW ON EARTH

charge of this new challenge.

In 1950 as the second half of the 20th century opened that August, the first Edinburgh Tattoo, produced by Lieutenant Colonel George Malcolm was held on the Esplanade of Edinburgh Castle.

The initial advertising was suitably restrained 'An Edinburgh Tattoo will take place on the Castle Esplanade at 10pm each evening from August 21 to September 9, Sundays excepted.' But the show would far outdo that understated expectation, largely because, by one of those happy quirks of fate, it was in exactly the right hands.

George Malcolm was one of those remarkable people in whom a number of talents came together at the right moment. He was the hereditary Chief of the Malcolms, so he had a deep sense of Scottish history in his veins. The Army had taught him Highland dancing to a professional standard and after a spell as a staff officer he had become a first-class administrator. His mother Jeanne was the daughter of the celebrated Edwardian actress Lillie Langtry and his

The 1952 Tattoo programme.

sister Mary was one of the first television announcers, so he was also born with a flair for show business which he had already shown at the 1938 Aldershot Tattoo.

The first Tattoo in Edinburgh had eight items and attracted an audience of 100,000 people over its 20 performances, 18 'normal' evening shows, one Saturday afternoon event and a special midnight performance to allow the people taking part in other Festival events to come up the hill and see the show. By that time small scaffolding stands had been added for the spectators and the tradition of volunteer stewards and Boy Scouts selling

The skirl of the pipes drifts over the city from the Castle Esplanade.

programmes had begun.

It ended in spectacular fashion with Her Majesty Queen Elizabeth (later the Queen Mother) and her daughter Princess Margaret attending on the final night. They saw the legendary Sir Thomas Beecham conducting the combined military bands of the Royal Scots, the Royal Scots Greys, the 9th Queen's Royal Lancers and the Highland Light Infantry, with the addition of eight double basses from the Royal Philharmonic Orchestra, in George Frederick Handel's Music for the Royal Fireworks which had the thunderous addition of 25-pounder guns fired from Mills Mount in the Castle.

The Lone Piper became a fixture from the start. The first Lone Piper was Pipe Major George Stoddart who played in every performance for the first eleven years and whose son Gavin was to follow in his father's footsteps as a Lone Piper and also to become Director of Army Bagpipe Music and Highland Drumming.

In 1950 no-one in the City of Edinburgh or in the Army could have known that the fledgling Edinburgh Tattoo would easily outlast all the other great tattoos of the first half of the 20th century and become the greatest show of its kind in the world.

THE GREATEST SHOW ON EARTH

Youth took centre stage in 1951 and included a display of Highland dancing by the boys of Queen Victoria School at Dunblane, set up after the South African Wars for the children of Scottish servicemen. The audience swelled to 160,000.

After those first two spectacular years, Lieutenant Colonel George Malcolm decided to step down to devote himself to running his Highland estate. Fortunately for the Tattoo, George Malcolm had had the able assistance of Lieutenant Colonel Alasdair Maclean CBE as Director, but as a serving Army officer he was not free to take over, so the Tattoo had the good fortune to have the services of Captain Forbes Taylor, a former Black Watch Officer as Producer for the third year. He had already helped George Malcolm with a 'Services Cavalcade' in Glasgow in 1938 and later went on to a successful career in film and television production.

A more momentous change in 1952 was the sudden death of King George VI and the accession of Her Majesty the Queen, Elizabeth II. Since then the Edinburgh Tattoo can say proudly that it has played on the Esplanade of Edinburgh Castle in every year of Her Majesty's historic reign.

That year, which showed the changes in the dress of the Scottish regiments over the previous 50 years, Forbes Taylor also introduced the first overseas performers to the Tattoo, the Royal Military Band of the Netherlands Army, the French Republican Guard Mounted Band and the pipes and drums of the Cameron Highlanders of Canada.

The Tattoo's former Director, Alasdair Maclean of Pennycross left the Army with the rank of Brigadier and immediately took over the production of the first Tattoo following the Coronation of Queen Elizabeth in 1953. A number of the bands which had taken part in the Coronation procession were on parade to the delight of the audience.

A natural showman, Brigadier Alasdair Maclean took over the commentary. He also set about attracting more overseas acts to beat a path to Edinburgh. In tandem with the Festival, the Tattoo was becoming more international, attracting an increasing number of acts and audiences to Edinburgh from abroad. He even took the show to Copenhagen in 1955. More importantly he understood that there was more to a military tattoo than bands and soldiers marching up and down and he introduced a greater variety of acts with country dancing, gymnastics, fire-fighting, motorcycle displays and 007 James Bond's Aston Martin which in turn attracted larger and larger audiences.

The Tattoo has never been stuffy. In 1962 Chubby Checker's 'Let's Twist Again' was still riding high in the charts and in that year's finale bandsmen encouraged people to come out of the stands and on to the Esplanade to do the Twist. People of all ages responded and on the ground and in the stands they danced.

Then after 13 strenuous years Brigadier Alasdair Maclean stood down, leaving a legacy which has long outlived him. He had carried on what George Malcolm and he had created in 1950 and built the Edinburgh Tattoo into a world-class event.

The search was on for a successor and retired Brigadier Jack Sanderson, a jovial former Scots Guards officer who had previously been Brigadier Alasdair Maclean's assistant, took up the challenge in 1968.

Although the Tattoo had already been seen on television for some years, it burst into full colour in 1968. By then the actor Tom Fleming was firmly established as the voice of the Tattoo on the BBC, although Jack Sanderson continued the tradition of the Producer announcing the acts on the Esplanade.

The Norwegian King's Guard established a lasting link with Edinburgh and the Tattoo in 1972 when it adopted one of the penguins at Edinburgh Zoo, named it Nils Olav after the Guard's commander Major Nils Egelien and His Majesty King Olav and bestowed upon it the rank of Lance Corporal. The penguin is promoted each time the King's Guard comes to Edinburgh and is now Commander in Chief of the King's Guard.

In 1975 the old scaffolding stands were replaced by stands built using a new German construction technique. These served the show and

Fireworks over Edinburgh Castle.

the public well for the next 36 years, although as people became generally larger the seats stayed the same size. This inevitably led to some grumbling – but not about the quality of the show.

The following year, in 1976 Jack Sanderson was succeeded as Producer by Lieutenant Colonel Leslie Dow OBE, a courageous former Cameronian, who had left the Army shortly after his Regiment had chosen disbandment rather than amalgamation. Leslie had organised the final parade of his Regiment on 28 May 1968 at Douglas Dale in Lanarkshire where it had been raised 279 years earlier.

On his arrival at the Tattoo he gave the old stones of Edinburgh Castle a voice. Each night he delivered a soliloquy in verse as the Castle reminded its audience of the turbulent sights it had seen and that it still stood steady on its ancient rock as the guardian of the Scottish capital.

At the end of the 1991 Tattoo Leslie Dow, who was more ill than many people realised, decided he would stand down as Producer. He had given some forewarning of his intention and the Tattoo Board had asked Major Michael Parker to shadow him.

How I Got the Job

MAJOR MICHAEL PARKER, who took on the mantle in 1992, had a formidable pedigree. He was a Queen's Own Hussar officer who had started by making his Officer's Mess dinner nights in Germany flamboyantly decorative before moving on to produce his first tattoo in Berlin and then the Royal Tournament in London as well as many very large Royal occasions.

As Michael, now Sir Michael, wrote in his autobiography *It's All Going Terribly Wrong*, 'In the past the Producer had always done the commentary. I certainly wasn't going to, so I looked around for a professional commentator.'

Michael did not know Scotland and the people in it and asked the late Tom Fleming, who had been narrating the BBC television productions of the Edinburgh Military Tattoo for many years. Tom was an actor and did not want to be tied down for four weeks during the Edinburgh International Festival and turned down Michael's kind offer.

So Michael turned to Ian Christie, who produced the BBC presentation, and asked him who else he could suggest. Ian, trying to be helpful, had a brainwave when he bumped into my brother Guthrie, who was the Senior Designer at the BBC in Scotland, and asked him what I was doing. As it happened it was not a lot and Guthrie gave him my contact details.

I had been a Member of the European Parliament for ten years up to 1989 when I lost my South of Scotland seat. Before that I had been an announcer with the BBC – mostly in Scotland, but also in Northern Ireland, London and Shetland. Ian remembered that, but more crucially he also remembered that I was a TA paratrooper and gave Michael my name.

In the spring of 1992 I had

a telephone call out of the blue from Michael's wonderfully able and patient assistant, Pixie Campbell MBE, who had spent 16 years in the Foreign Office before she returned to Edinburgh and became part of the small Tattoo team.

I was a bit taken aback but did not hesitate and replied at once, leaving a message that I would be delighted to come up to Edinburgh Castle to discuss the suggestion. The call had a sense of déjà vu as I had also had a message out of the blue in 1964 asking me to come

to the BBC for an audition to become an announcer.

I heard nothing for a couple of months and thought the Tattoo must have found someone else so I put the glorious idea out of my mind and pressed ahead with my freelance work giving the Royal Bank of Scotland and the Isle of Man Parliament, among others, my advice on European legislation.

Then Pixie broke cover again and said Michael would like to see me at 10.30am in the Conference Room

Alasdair Hutton at the microphone in the storyteller's box.

at Edinburgh Castle on 18 June. So up the hill I went and after a short, pleasant conversation, I was in. Michael was obviously more relaxed than I was. In his book he described the process.

'A TA officer called Alasdair Hutton was suggested. He had a splendid voice and was fun which fitted the job description perfectly.' You do not often get the chance to see yourself as others see you.

I thought he was taking a risk and he had cut it fine. I had not done anything like it before and the Tattoo production conference for the 1992 show was only 45 days away, with rehearsals starting the following day and the first show the Friday after that.

I had watched the Tattoo on television regularly and admired the presenters who had been invariably senior Army officers. I had thought that it would be a wonderful job to have, but never dreamed that one day I would be sitting high over the Esplanade telling people what was happening. Although, like most people, I had often seen the show on television, I realised with some horror that I had only once sat in the stands to watch it. I had a very steep learning curve ahead of me.

But of course this did have a huge advantage. After 18 years as a volunteer paratrooper I had accumulated some military understanding, I had some 15 years of broadcasting experience, ten years of speech-making as an MEP and no pre-conceived idea of how this world-famous Tattoo should be presented. So I had to start with a blank sheet.

Well, not quite blank. Michael had a wonderful scriptwriter whom he had used for some years on other shows so he produced a script, but few people notice that there is also a period of warm-up before the Tattoo to entertain, inform and involve the audience and a long string of thanks after the show. Leslie Dow had had the invaluable help in the box of identical twins Lieutenant Colonels Ian and Stuart McBain who had developed the pre-show 'entertainment' to a fine art but who retired along with Leslie.

Pixie gallantly showed me a copy of the warm-up which had gone before and I went to work to adapt it to my style and insert what I thought was essential to catch the attention of the audience and prepare them for the show to come.

Although he did not say so openly to me, Michael wanted to create a Tattoo which was different from the great Edinburgh Tattoos which had gained the show such a strong international reputation.

Leslie Dow had stamped his personality on the opening of the show as the Voice of the Castle and I thought it would be quite wrong to try to create another Voice of the Castle. Although we had never discussed it, Michael and I agreed that that must remain as a memorial to Leslie's great contribution to the Tattoo's success. It is still spoken of fondly to this day.

I love Scottish poetry so I began searching back through Scottish verses for something suitable to close the show after the Lone Piper. There was a wonderful array of work to read but it was fairly soon obvious that Sir Walter Scott's majestic lines from the last Canto of *The Lay of the Last Minstrel* could not be surpassed.

The dilemma lay in trimming them to suit the end of a great event. I asked the forgiveness of the shade of 'The Wizard of the North' and pressed together two small sections from the Canto to produce the lines with which I have closed the Tattoo in every year but one since 1992.

Breathes there the man
with soul so dead
Who never to
himself hath said
This is my own,
my native land.
Land of brown heath
and shaggy wood
Land of the mountain
and the flood
Land of my sires.
What mortal hand could
ere untie the filial band
That knits me to thy
rugged strand?

Then I added 'Scotland – Scotland the Brave' as the cue to the piece of music, now the Regimental March of the Royal Regiment of Scotland, with which the bands start to leave at the end of the show.

Only in 1996, when the Tattoo commemorated the 200th anniversary of the death of Robert Burns, did that vary when I used these lines from 'The Cotter's Saturday Night':

The lines are fine but do not capture for me the essence of my land in the way Sir Walter's do.

It was a coincidence, but a happy one, that I became a Life Member of the Edinburgh Sir Walter Scott Club in 1994 and much later, its Chairman.

Sir Walter Scott's lines resonate with many people and I am always cheered when foreign groups coming back to the Tattoo take pleasure in reciting to me the lines they have heard night after night, memorised and kept in their minds sometimes for years after the event.

I am touched that they take home something of the essence of the country in which they have spent a month working hard and entertaining the huge crowds and clearly treasure it.

I am sure Sir Walter would smile to think of his lines still going round the world all these years after he wrote them.

Alasdair Hutton getting ready for the show.

From scenes like these,
old Scotia's grandeur springs
That makes her lov'd at
home, rever'd abroad:
O Scotia, my dear,
my native soil!
Be blest with health, and
peace, and sweet content!
Scotland –
Scotland the brave!

THE GREATEST SHOW ON EARTH

1992–94
Major Michael Parker

I DO NOT remember feeling terrified or even nervous as I looked out at that big crowd on the first night on 7 August 1992, rather I recall feeling that I must not let down this great institution or the people who had come from across the world and bought tickets to see the show.

Having done virtually all my broadcasting live, having had to jump out of many aircraft on a precise command over 22 years, and having had to speak to the European Parliament when the President called was all excellent training for presenting the world's greatest Tattoo precisely on time. In a live show there are no hiding places, you have to get it right or everyone knows you have blundered.

Since 1975 the production team of the Producer, his assistant, the show caller, the narrator – as I chose to be called – plus the sound operator and the lighting operators were all crowded into one small 'pod' at the top of the East Stand.

We also enjoyed the company of a stream of visitors who were always agog with wonder at what was happening and were usually oblivious to the narrator trying to concentrate on the script and read the link to the next act at the right moment. Tuning out the idle chatter going on around me was just one more challenge to beat each night.

With the arrival of new stands in 2011 the narrator – now the storyteller – sits in a separate, larger pod with the sound team and the volume of chattering during the narration has thankfully dropped away.

After the first couple of years I took over the writing of the script completely and, prompted by the experience of these early distractions, started to add more and more detail to the accompanying instructions.

That way if anyone was unwise enough to distract me at a critical moment I could always find out where I should be quickly and accurately. I do not think the audience has ever been aware of any of these moments but there have been occasions when I have been very glad to have all these detailed signposts to get me back on track.

I had the benefit of knowing the way in which previous Tattoos on the Esplanade had been introduced but after the first year I felt that the audience needed small changes to warm it up to be fully ready for the show each night. There was nothing dramatic but gradual steps added small things.

Instead of asking from which towns people had come, I moved to countries as our international audiences grew bigger. I finished each night by pitting the cheers of the Scots in friendly rivalry against the cheers from the English, which seemed to amuse the audiences.

There had always been welcomes to individuals but I managed to expand this, discovering how much people love to hear their names in public and make it clear to everyone around them that I had just welcomed them.

As the cult of the selfie arose this played very well

The Turkish Mehter Band appearing in the 1992 Tattoo.

with people who get very excited at having their names called out, and on many nights I wondered if I would manage to mention everyone who asked before we had to start the show.

In 1994 I used the practice of singing 'Happy Birthday' as part of the welcome to everyone in the audience celebrating a birthday that night. But when I say 'singing', I mean that I asked the audience to sing because I am a poor singer. My idea was that if the audience would sing and drown me out it would not only be more pleasant for them but it would also make them feel part of the show and not just passive spectators.

That was proved one night when a young singer with one of the bands asked if she could sing 'Happy Birthday' to one of her friends in the audience. She sang it beautifully but of course the audience listened to her singing, did not get involved and were rather slower to become enthusiastic about the show that night.

That year I also added a section in my introduction telling the visitors about Scottish inventions and discoveries and about some of our most distinguished and clever, if not always well-known, Scots. Sadly that has been squeezed out by more recent changes to the way the show is introduced but I was rather proud of being able to tell our visitors about our achievements down the years.

There is one set of 'shout-outs' I have always enjoyed doing but still remain puzzled about after 25 years and those are the proposals of marriage I am asked to make for other people.

Every year someone, men and women, will ask if I can propose marriage on their behalf to their prospective spouse. I have not quite understood why but I quite accept that to make their declaration even by proxy in front of several thousand people is a memorable way to start their lives together.

I try to identify where they are sitting and ask the spotlight operators to highlight the happy couple. I recall one young lady who was so keen to make sure that she was there and in good time to have the question popped to her boyfriend that they were among the first people there and sat alone in the vast, empty stand for some time before the other seats filled up around them.

1992

In those first years of Michael Parker's control the show became much more theatrical, with clear historical themes each year. In 1992 the raising of the Scots Guards was woven together with the early beginnings of military music in Britain.

Music had echoed from the Turkish Ottoman Empire and the gloriously costumed Mehter Band from Turkey brought it to life, not just with their clearly oriental music but their wholly unexpected style of marching, taking two steps forward, turning half right, turning back and after two more steps turning half left. Michael augmented this historical element with a small Scots Guard band in 18th-century costume and playing some of the instruments from the period, including a Jingling Johnny and a Serpent.

But the finale of the 1992 Tattoo will remain memorable for introducing the tune 'Highland Cathedral' to the wider world. It was already ten years old and Michael had it arranged for a band and pipes in Berlin, where it was composed, but it had not attracted any serious attention. But Michael believed in it and the 1992 finale proved him right. From then on the piece never looked back and is now one of the most famous and popular pipe tunes around the world.

1993

Michael loved fire and introduced the gas braziers and torchères which have blazed every night at every Tattoo since 1992 in front of and on the Castle ramparts. He also used fire in the shows and in 1993 the show started with a blazing Viking longboat introducing the story of Royal Scotland from the early chieftains to the State Visit of King George IV in 1822. In that year Michael also introduced amateur actors to tell the story.

In each show there were always the hugely popular staples of the massed pipes and drums and the Highland dancers. The former World Champion Billy Forsyth had been steadily developing the young dancers, who would soon show just how far they

had come under his careful and imaginative guidance.

We always have a 'preview' night to which the press and broadcasters come, along with an audience which buys tickets at half price, and they give us a very good guide to how the audience will react to the show. Of course no two audiences are exactly alike, but I started to develop an instinct for the mood of the audience on each night and

tried to alter the tone of the narration to suit that mood.

1994
1994 marked the 200th and last birthday of the Gordon Highlanders, before they were amalgamated with the Queen's Own Highlanders to form the Highlanders. The tableau not only included a recruiting kiss from Duchess of Gordon but a vignette of the Gordons' part in the Battle of Waterloo.

The finale of the 1993 Tattoo.

'Brewitt and Leggitt still in business', an entre-act celebrating 500 years of distilling whisky in Scotland.

Each night the audience rather ungallantly cheered each time a French soldier theatrically fell dead, which did not go down well with the French Consul-General when he attended. Audiences can be wonderful but fickle too.

Sometimes even performers, and military performers at that, can be equally unpredictable. The 1994 Tattoo also celebrated the 500th anniversary of the first distilling of whisky with a whimsical, little entre-act in which a portable still carrying the legend 'Brewitt and Leggitt still in business' was wheeled on to the Esplanade by a couple of 'Highlanders'. They were arrested by Redcoats who could not resist tasting a dram themselves. Overcome by the effects of the whisky they were no match for the next group of Highlanders, who booted them off the Esplanade while their colleagues triumphantly recovered the still.

But one night no Highlanders came to their colleagues' rescue. I had to think fast and so did the Highlanders pulling the still. I kept the narration going and the Highlanders got the message and kept the still going until it disappeared from sight. Happily the audience was none the wiser – but the leader of the rescuing Highlanders, who had missed his cue while he was chatting up some girls at

THE GREATEST SHOW ON EARTH

the bottom of the Esplanade, learned a swift form of Army wisdom that night.

Before the Tattoo that year, at the end of May came the sad but memorable farewell concert by the Band of the Royal Scots Dragoon Guards in the Usher Hall before it was disbanded to save money. This was the band which had accompanied the Pipes and Drums of the Regiment in their number one hit single of 'Amazing Grace'.

The concert was memorable for the stunning appearance of the Dire Straits guitarist Mark Knopfler not only playing his own 'Going Home' from the film set in Scotland *Local Hero* but also 'Amazing Grace' with the band and the Pipes and Drums. It was also memorable for bringing together the talents of Michael Parker, the man who would be the next Producer of the Tattoo, Brigadier Melville Jameson, who had been the Pipe President of the regiment's pipes and drums when they made their hit record and also Major David Allfrey, then Commanding C Squadron in the Regiment who would become the Tattoo Producer in 2011.

The concert was spectacular. It recalled highlights of the Regiment's long and continuing history, and it was moving to present, but sadly the Regiment was not allowed to advertise so the Hall was a long way from being filled.

While he was producing the Royal Tournament, after the concert and just before the Tattoo that year Michael had a stroke.

It gave him a bad fright and he came to the rehearsals looking ill and subdued. But he had already prepared the show so the team that he had gathered closed ranks and, with the Business Manager, Major Brian Leishman, holding the reins, we presented what was to be Michael's final Edinburgh Tattoo.

It was almost mine as well. During the 1994 Tattoo I was working in Aberdeen giving people who had lost their jobs advice on how to get back into work. That meant I had to drive to Edinburgh every evening and then back again at night for a month. It was gruelling but, feeling a debt of honour to Michael and the instinct that the show must go on, I did it.

The following year, to my horror and quite late in the day, my colleague in the office decided she would go on holiday in August and after the experience of the previous year I thought briefly about giving up narrating the Tattoo. Driving up and down each night was potentially lethal but I had grown to really enjoy the big show on the Esplanade, so I called on the Airborne spirit, gritted my teeth, learned the location of every layby between Dundee and Aberdeen where I could snatch a hasty nap and managed to reach the Castle each night and did not miss a show.

As the season went on I grew more tired each night. Driving down was not a problem. I would leave Aberdeen at 4.30pm in daylight but at the end of the show I was still exhilarated by the show and only came down from the 'high' slowly. It had usually gone by the stretch between Perth and Dundee and the rest of the drive north of Dundee became a tougher and tougher challenge every night as I fought to stay alert and often drew in to a layby for a quick ten-minute nap to make me sharp enough to reach Aberdeen in one piece. As I look back it was one of the hardest things I have ever done but facing the challenge and winning was well worth it.

1995–99
Brigadier Melville Jameson

IN 1995 BRIGADIER Melville Jameson, known universally as Mel, took over the Tattoo helm. He had been Pipe President of the SCOTS DGS when they achieved the unexpected accolade of six weeks at number one in the hit parade with 'Amazing Grace' in 1972. So he had military and musical credentials and steered the show away from the historical tableaux towards a more musical Tattoo.

Tattoos and their acts are usually booked and prepared sometimes two or three years in advance, so Mel inherited the tribute to the Royal Stewart dynasty in Scotland. He also inherited the Egyptian Military Musical Group or Group 101, as it had been called when it was formed of 100 musicians and their Director. Leading the Band out each night was its Drum Major, Mohammed, who was the strongest man at handling a Drum Major's mace that I have ever seen. He could spin the mace one-handed with either hand and with a seemingly gentle flick of his forearm could send the nearly one-kilogramme

The Egyptian Military Musical Group.

mace high into the air.

The Egyptians came with a full-sized chariot from the era of the great Rameses II, who ruled Egypt from 1279 to 1213 BCE. In the chariot, pulled of course by 'slaves', stood a character dressed as Rameses but almost more spectacular were the swaggering bagpipers. Someone, possibly a Scot with a sense of humour, must have told them that a piper needed to swagger a bit to swing his kilt but the Egyptian pipers had taken swaggering to a new level.

I had always tried to find a thread which linked the acts so Mel challenged me to come up with a link between the Egyptian Pharaohs and the Stewart kings. By one of those chances which make writing and researching such fun, I found just what I was looking for in an old tale. Although they had come to Scotland from France, the Stewarts always claimed a far older ancestry. They boasted that they were descended from Scota, the daughter of an Egyptian Pharaoh. True or not, it was a good story and a superb link.

Also playing that year was the *Musique du 42 Regiment de Transmissions*, the band of a French Signals Regiment, billed in the programme as one of France's most prestigious military bands. Heading the French band was Drum Major Jean-Marie Pichon. Drum Major Pichon was quite short but was obviously determined not to be outdone by his Egyptian counterpart. On the last performance both Drum Majors seemed to engage in a mace-throwing contest as they marched down the Esplanade for the finale. Higher and higher went each mace but, probably dazzled by the powerful lights, the Egyptian Drum Major's mace slipped from his grasp on its final descent, which must have made the French Drum Major feel smug.

The Tattoo team has always been able to turn its hand to presenting other ceremonial events and during the 1995 Tattoo, it produced the main Scottish ceremonial event to mark VJ Day (Victory over Japan) on the evening of Sunday 20 August.

This was a fine challenge, as it was necessary to create the right atmosphere and also run the event to precise timings to meet the requirements of a United Kingdom-wide live broadcast and maintain a continuous ceremony for the audience around the Esplanade. That was made tricky by the BBC constantly moving the time at which it planned to include the Scottish segment.

The BBC wanted to come to Edinburgh to catch the moment the massed pipes and drums marched out over the drawbridge. Writing the script, I realised that we would need a flexible buffer which also kept the show flowing on the Esplanade so I wrote an account of the surrender of the Imperial Japanese forces, carefully broken into ten-second-long sentences. By doing that, as we approached the constantly moving opt point I was able to give the audience in Edinburgh an accurate account of the surrender, then at the right moment jump to the sentence which wrapped it up and introduce the pipes and drums so that they started playing and marching at the very moment the BBC showed them appearing on the drawbridge.

As it happened, switching between UK and Scottish programmes on television was the sort of thing I had done as a BBC announcer many times so it was relatively easy but still a little nerve-wracking doing it with a team who had never done this sort of thing before and had no rehearsal. On the night it worked without either the live or the television audiences realising the fine line between getting it just right and making an obvious mess of it.

1996
There was a change of gear in 1996 when the Tattoo decided to commemorate the bi-centenary of the death of Robert Burns. I had been speaking and reciting at Burns Suppers for nearly 30 years by then so it was a pleasurable task to create a script which told the story of Burns' life using quotations from his verses.

I asked an old colleague from the BBC, Alec Monteath, who was an accomplished and much sought-after Burns reciter, and well known as Dugald Lachlan the shepherd in the long-running television series *Take the High Road*, to record the snippets of verse. Alec was superb and brought the lines to life. Youngsters

Kwa Zulu Natal Police dancers.

portrayed a host of favourite Burns characters and Burns himself. Tam was mounted on horseback and the witch nicknamed 'Cutty-sark' became adept at snatching at the horse's rump and waving a tail as Tam vanished over the drawbridge into the dark.

But there was good Tattoo variety mixed with the Burns poetry as well. There were the startlingly effective South African Police Zulu drummers who used pieces of plastic pipe instead of drumsticks and created a thunderous sound which brought home how chilling it must have been for the British soldiers facing the might of the Zulu nation in the 19th century.

Although Burns had been a Volunteer soldier, he would never have matched the dazzling brilliance of the weapon handling of The Old Guard – the United States Army Drill Team, which also took part. For the first time, the finest military band in America from Washington, DC – the United States Army Band, Pershing's Own, under Colonel

The United States Army Drill Team.

Bryan Shelburne Junior – appeared at the Tattoo.

1997

The Golden Wedding Anniversary year of Her Majesty the Queen and Prince Philip fell in 1997. It was also the United Kingdom Year of the Commonwealth. Her Majesty is, of course, head of the Commonwealth so the Tattoo welcomed performers from four Commonwealth countries. We had the Rats of Tobruk and the Western Australia Police pipe bands from Australia, the Lochiel Marching Team from New Zealand, the forces' champion pipes and drums of the 8th Independent Kashmir Regiment from Pakistan with the Khyber Rifles Khattak dancers and the warmth and colour of the British Caribbean islands with the newly formed Trinidad and Tobago Defence Force Steel Orchestra and Drums making their first appearance at Edinburgh. The brainchild of Brigadier General Carlton Alfonso, the Chief of the Trinidad and Tobago Defence Staff, who saw the group as superb ambassadors for the islands, they marched on crisply in three ranks and

The Royal Marines abseil fron the Castle.

then took the Tattoo by storm breaking away with their exuberant style of playing and dancing to all corners of the Esplanade led by their Drum Major Sergeant Rufus Lewis.

It was also the Year of the Seafarer and the Kings Squad of Her Majesty's Royal Marines showed their skill on the parade ground,

The Trinidad and Tobago Defence Force Steel Band make their debut at the Tattoo.

The King's Squad
of Her Majesty's
Royal Marines.

while the Comacchio Group
from Arbroath 'helicoptered
in' to thwart an armed and
dangerous gang attempting
the steal the Honours of
Scotland – the Scottish Crown

Jewels – from the Castle.

1997 also saw the start of a
move towards contemporary
Highland dancing, with
the dancers being escorted
on by kilted warriors with

Left: The Trinidad
and Tobago
Defence Force
Drum Major
Rufus Lewis.
Right: The Drum
Major of the
8th Independent
Kashmir Regiment.

flaming torches and the dance growing from the great traditions of Scotland to a modern heritage of music and dance. I described it as 'a style and a design for a new generation' in the Tattoo Ceilidh Dance which produced some remarkable dancing and some extraordinary piping from the late Pipe Major Alasdair Gillies.

This was also the 25th anniversary of the SCOTS DGS' number one hit with 'Amazing Grace', so with the man who had been the Regiment's Pipe President in 1972 now being the Tattoo Producer it was just the right moment to mark the anniversary with Pipe Major Bryon Brotherton

of the RSDG and Pipe Major Steven Small of the Black Watch, who was to go on to become a future Director of Army Bagpipe Music.

1998

1998 was a remarkable year for anniversaries, the centenary of the Royal Army Medical Corps, the 80th anniversary of the Formation of the Royal Air Force and the ending of the First World War, the 60th anniversary of the founding of the Women's Royal Voluntary Service and the Auxiliary Territorial Service, which were both raised in 1938.

The Tattoo fielded the largest number of pipers and

One of the Australian pipers.

Royal Marines in their Arctic gear.

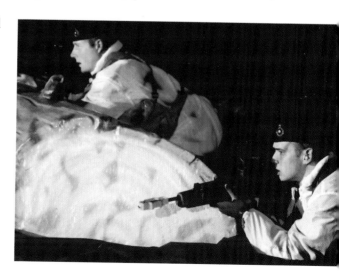

The Imps motorcycle display team.

drummers it had seen up to then and an even bigger noise from the remarkable Imps motorcycle display team appearing on the Esplanade for the third time.

This team is an extraordinary tribute to the tenacity of its founder Roy Pratt MBE who put it together in the East End of London in 1972 with the aim of helping youngsters from the area, both boys and girls, to grow up, to get the most from their education and to divert them from getting into trouble with the authorities.

The youngsters, who range from six up to 16, demonstrate quite remarkable skills on their various sizes of motorbikes and throw in comedy as well. They can be mischievous on and off the Esplanade, but the thrill of performing at a show such as Edinburgh and in other sometimes exotic locations has kept them on the straight and narrow and turned out a string of success stories from its members over the years.

I enjoyed working with Roy and the youths and got to know them well during the course of the rehearsals

Fijian Meke dancers.

and the show. I obviously did not know it at the time, but it was to lead to several events together in other places away from the Tattoo.

1998 also provided superb contrasts with the City of Dunedin and the City of Invercargill Caledonian Pipe Bands from New Zealand celebrating the 150th anniversary of the founding of their very Scottish communities, the Fiji Military Forces Band and its Meke Warrior Dancers, the Scottish country dancers, the Central Band of the Russian Navy which owed much of its early influence to Scottish Admirals and the Band of the Coldstream Guards.

It was also the year in which the Tattoo programme began to grow in size from its A5 format (5½ inches by 8½ inches) to 6½ inches by 9½ inches. Most other big events used A4 sized programmes but Edinburgh remained modest.

1999
Then in 1999 we reached the 50th Edinburgh Military Tattoo. No other Tattoo had run that long and I do not know if any of the folk who had then faith to embark on the first Edinburgh Tattoo in 1950 had envisaged it achieving that, but it had and there we were to prove it.

To celebrate, the Tattoo had a new tartan designed by Lieutenant Colonel Peter MacDonald, a leading tartan scholar. The new tartan was based on the original 'government tartan' from the 18th century and, adding the red of the less well known 'band tartan' and a black stripe which represents the City of Edinburgh, the new tartan was a colourful addition to the 'branding' of the Tattoo.

The main focus of the final Tattoo of the 20th century was the 200th anniversary of the raising of the 93rd Sutherland Highlanders, the Regiment that had been immortalised as The Thin Red Line after its action against Russian cavalry at the Battle of Balaklava in 1854.

The normal formation in which infantry met a cavalry charge at that time was to form a square, but Sir Colin Campbell formed the Highlanders into two lines instead of the customary four. The *Times* correspondent William Russell had said that he could see nothing in front of the charging Russians but the 'thin red streak tipped with a line of steel' of the 93rd. The phrase was shortened to 'the thin red line' and has passed into the language as a symbol of British composure in battle.

There was a small irony that the Tattoo opened with the tune 'Preobajensky', named after the famous Russian regiment of Foot Guards, but it gave a perfect opportunity to show off two well-loved drum horses, Leonidas of the Life Guards and the magnificent Ramillies of the SCOTS DG, named for the Duke of Marlborough's victory over the French at the battle of Ramillies in 1706. Affectionately known to the soldiers as Rambo, he was presented to the Regiment by Her Majesty the Queen in May 1987 and was received by Lieutenant Colonel Mel Jameson, then Commanding the Regiment and in 1999 the Producer of the Tattoo. Leonidas was carrying two kettle drums presented to the Regiment in May 1831 by King William IV, each weighing 80 pounds.

The Tattoo went on to pay tribute to the actions of the regiments which came together in 1881 as the Argyll and Sutherland Highlanders, including its historic action in 1967 when the Regiment re-established control of the Crater district of Aden under Lieutenant Colonel Colin Mitchell with

Moko Jumbies from Barbados, with six-year-old Shaquil Best.

Shaggy Bear, the spirit of life. Because the Moko Jumbies were up at the height of the audiences in the stands they were able to reach out and shake hands, which delighted the people they reached.

To maintain the juxtaposition of styles which the Tattoo manages to bring together every year, we also welcomed one of the most flamboyant and sought-after of all the American university bands – from the Southeast Missouri State University in the land of the mighty Mississippi River – the Golden Eagles, directed by Professor Barry Bernhardt. The band created a wonderful and popular spectacle with their dancers, flag and baton throwers, and the special skills of 19-year-old Erin Fluegge, known as Fliggy, with her flaming batons.

Fliggy – Erin Fluegge – with her flaming batons.

Earlier in the programme we had watched the graceful flow of the Scottish country dances with their elegant reminder of the days when Scotland and France were closely bound in the Auld Alliance. As they danced away to the 'Monaghan Jig' we did not know that it would be the last time the

maximum efficiency and minimum bloodshed.

In complete contrast the Barbados Defence Force Band brought from with them the Caribbean the spirit of the African heritage of the islands with the stilt-walking Moko Jumbie dancers, who included six-year-old Shaquil Best, and down on the ground was the colourful Mother Sally, the spirit of fertility, and

The Golden Eagles from Southeast Missouri State University.

country dancers would appear at the Edinburgh Tattoo. Later in the show we were to witness the extraordinary Highland dancing of the Australasian Champion and new British Champion Amy Martin from McLean in Northern New South Wales dancing to the drumming of Corporal Neil Sloan of the Argyll and Sutherland Highlanders and the athletic dancing of the Tattoo Ceilidh Dancers around her.

In 1950 the Mounted Band of the Life Guards had appeared in the first Edinburgh Tattoo so it was right to ask them to return for the 50th Edinburgh Military Tattoo. They were joined by all the other British cavalry

The three drum horses on the show.

bands – the Hussars and Light Dragoons, just back from Kosovo, Dragoon Guards, Royal Lancers and the Royal Tank Regiment, all entirely appropriate for a producer whose service was in the

The Life Guards
Drum horse Leonidas. The Life Guards drum horses are named after classical Greek heroes and carry solid silver kettle drums weighing 80lbs each. The were originally presented by H.M. King William IV in May 1831.

The Royal Scots Dragoon Guards
Drum horse Ramillies or 'Rambo' as the soldiers of the Regiment like to call him, is the drum horse of The Royal Scots Dragoon Guards. He is a black horse of 18 hands in size and was presented to the Regiment by H.M. The Queen. The presentation took place at the Windsor Horse Show in May 1987.

The Queen's Royal Hussars
Regimental drum horse, Peninsula, was presented to The Queen's Royal Hussars by H.M. Queen Elizabeth, The Queen Mother. The drum horse, carrying kettle drums decorated with their battle honours, always parades at the head of the Regiment on ceremonial and state occasions.

THE GREATEST SHOW ON EARTH

Scottish country dancers.

Scottish cavalry regiment.

In 1650 the Scottish Parliament ordered the raising of a Mounted Regiment of Life Guards for King Charles II. It was dispersed after the disastrous Battle of Worcester but in 1661 another troop of Horse Guards was raised in Scotland for the King and they moved to London with the Act of Union in 1707. The Band uniform of the Life Guards is the oldest British ceremonial dress, dating back to the time of King Charles II, and permission to wear it comes from Her Majesty the Queen. So it was not only right but spectacular to end the 20th century with this historic unit on parade in Edinburgh.

The 1999 Tattoo also left the new century an enduring legacy in selling every seat for the first time. It was a practice which was to become a habit in all the subsequent shows in the 21st century.

2000–06
Brigadier Melville Jameson

The Tattoo's Golden Jubilee programme 2000.

The programme for Scotland's Tribute to Her Majesty Queen Elizabeth the Queen Mother's 100th birthday.

THE NEW MILLENNIUM started with a trip to New Zealand in March where the Tattoo played to sell out crowds at the Westpac Stadium in Wellington. But I shall say a little more about that in the Ninth Act.

Four months later, on 27 July, the week before the main Tattoo, the Tattoo Production Team presented a Beating Retreat on the Esplanade of the Castle as Scotland's Royal Tribute to celebrate the 100th birthday of Queen Elizabeth the Queen Mother, which would fall eight days later on the first night of the Tattoo.

The event attracted the most high-powered group of guests who had attended a Tattoo event: five members of the Royal Family, the senior officers of the Services in Scotland, Government and civic leaders and representatives of the Scottish and United Kingdom parliaments, the

Commonwealth and many local organisations. All of them were received by Brigadier Hughie Monro, commander of the 52nd Brigade, whose headquarters were in Edinburgh Castle.

As well as the country's tribute to the Queen Mother, the evening would also raise money for Erskine Hospital. They needed to build modern facilities in the grounds of the old hospital in Renfrewshire to ensure that it could continue to look after the wounded servicemen and women in its care.

The event gathered the largest Massed Pipes and Drums ever seen on the Esplanade of Edinburgh Castle with the pipe bands of all the Scottish Regiments in the British Army, the Royal Ghurkha Rifles, two Territorial Army pipes and drums and pipe bands representing eight affiliated regiments from the Commonwealth along with the band of the Scots Guards, the Lowland and Highland Bands of the Scottish Division and the Territorial Army Bands of 51st Highland Brigade and 52nd Lowland Brigade and dancers from Queen Victoria School, Dunblane, all under the Director of Music from the Scots Guards, Major Bob Owen.

The musical programme had a clear Royal bias including a tribute written specially for the performance by the Director of Army Bagpipe Music, Major Gavin Stoddart MBE, BEM, – 'Scotland's Salute to Queen Elizabeth the Queen Mother' and 'When the Pipers Play', which was written for the Queen Mother for her 100th birthday.

A full and enthusiastic audience gave three resounding cheers which bounced back from the Castle walls before they sang 'For She's a Jolly Good Fellow' to round off the evening.

The Tattoo moved up to a glossy A4-sized programme for that event and followed it with a similar-sized gold-coloured programme for its Golden Jubilee performances in August.

Not only was the 2000 Tattoo the first of the new Millennium in front of the Castle, but it was also the Tattoo's Golden Jubilee and by chance the Golden Jubilee of the Commonwealth as well so the show opened with a new fanfare 'Salute to The Commonwealth' and the whole show took on a clearly Commonwealth flavour.

We welcomed the Ngati Rangiwewehi Maori Group from New Zealand, who celebrated the Great Maori Canoe Migration with

Ngati Rangiwewehi Maori Group.

a Poi Dance, an action song, and the fearsome war dance – the Haka.

From Canada came the Royal Canadian Mounted Police, the inspiration for which came from the country's first Prime Minister, the Scots-born Sir John A. MacDonald in 1873.

From South Africa came the Zulu warriors of 121 Battalion South African Infantry under their Chief Corporal Simon Nduna. They demonstrated the fearsome shield slapping and singing with which they had confronted the

A young Cook Islands dancer.

soldiers of Queen Victoria in years gone by.

South Australia began to be settled in 1836 but numerous Aboriginal tribes had already lived there for thousands of years. So from Australia came the Anarungga Aboriginal Dance Company with Paaroo Michael Harris using boomerangs and Robert Nukhanwoldi with the *yidarki* or didgeridoo bidding us an aboriginal welcome. They were joined by the Band and Callisthenic Dancers of the South Australia Police with their giant Kangaroo, Adelaide, and its Joey, Glenelg, in a thoroughly Australian programme.

The Trinidad and Tobago Defence Force Steel Orchestra and Drums came to represent the Caribbean territories playing well known West Indian tunes before they marched off to 'Wi A Hundred Pipers' to the appreciative cheers of the big audience.

Of course the United Kingdom was represented by the pipers and drummers, the Highland dancers and the Band of HM Royal Marines from Rosyth, the Band of the Scots Guards and the Highland and Lowland

Bands from Scotland to send the Tattoo into the new Millennium in style.

2001

After such a hectic year in 2000, Brigadier Jameson steadied the ship in 2001 with a more traditional line-up of pipes and drums, Highland dancers and a judicious mixture of old and new visitors.

We welcomed back His Majesty the King of Norway's remarkable Guard. What makes them extraordinary is that these are young conscripts serving one year of military service – but anyone who has watched them would not guess it from their immaculate drill and impeccable musicianship. They are a constant tribute to the skill of their officers and senior NCOs who manage to bring them to a high pitch of perfection every year. We were also glad to see again the Emerald Isle Irish Dance Team who joined the Tattoo's Ceilidh Dancers in a specially choreographed Celtic Dance display which, of course, included Lord of the Dance. And, not to be left out, the Tattoo also welcomed the Regimental mascot of the

Russian Cossacks.

Royal Irish Regiment, the two-and-a-half-year-old Irish wolfhound Brian Boru the Seventh with his handler Corporal Brian Davidson.

The other two groups could hardly have been more different, the Russian Cossack State Song and Dance Ensemble and the Cook Islands National Youth Dance Team from Polynesia in the South Pacific.

The Cook Islands dancers were specially formed for the 2001 Tattoo from the country's three main high schools. I think everyone who saw the teenage boys and girls and their young drummers must have sympathised with

A singer from Cook Islands.

them when the cold wind blew across the Esplanade and the occasional shower fell. The costumes were grass skirts with only a light further covering above them, leaving the girls quite exposed to the vagaries of what we like to call the summer in Scotland as they brought us their traditional Cook Island welcome 'Kia Orana'.

By contrast, the Russian Cossacks were warmly clad from head to toe as they gave the crowd an energetic display of Cossack dancing and singing. The old Cossacks, who were spread along the southern borders of Russia, were remarkably similar to the old Scottish Borderers as a fiercely independent and unruly race with their own unique culture and folklore. Many distinguished Scottish soldiers fought in the ranks of the Cossacks and their first non-Cossack *Ataman* or Chief was a descendant of the Hamilton family. In the 19th century, the Cossacks attracted the great

A group of the Cook Islands dancers.

THE GREATEST SHOW ON EARTH

A traditional Cossack dance from southern Russia.

admiration of Sir Walter Scott for their implacable opposition to the French Emperor Napoleon and their relentless efforts to capture him.

But it would not have been a complete Tattoo if we had not recognised something particularly Scottish and in 2001 it was the heroism of the pipers and drummers of the regiments which had come together to form the Highlanders Regiment.

There was the staggering courage of Piper Kenneth Mackay of the 79th Cameron Highlanders at the Battle of Waterloo in 1815 when he stepped outside the bayonets of his comrades'

square and defiantly played the pipes in the face of the advancing French cavalry. King George III was so moved by his courage that he presented him with a silver-mounted set of pipes.

Pipers also left their mark on the North West frontier of India in 1897. As the Gordon Highlanders attacked the Heights of Dargai, Piper George Findlater achieved lasting fame and a Victoria Cross for gallantry when he was shot in both feet but continued to encourage his comrades by playing his pipes until the chanter was smashed by an Afghan bullet.

But it was not only the

A Cossack singer.

pipers who were heroic – the drummers too showed remarkable courage. At the Battle of the Somme in 1916 Drummer Walter Ritchie, a 2nd Seaforth, stood on the parapet of an enemy trench and repeatedly sounded The Charge to rally men who were wavering under heavy machine gun fire and bomb attacks. He too won a Victoria Cross for his immense bravery.

2002

2002 dawned as the Golden Jubilee year of Her Majesty the Queen's reign. There were celebrations of the Jubilee around the country and the Tattoo joined in with a programme to fit the occasion.

I am old enough to remember the shock the country felt at the unexpected death of King George VI in February 1952 and the surge of interest which immediately followed at the accession of his daughter as Queen. She was a young woman on tour in Kenya with her husband when her father died and the machinery of State moved smoothly into motion to proclaim the new monarch.

I had already spent quite a lot of time in libraries making

sure that I knew exactly what had been said where, when and by whom. I was able to open the Tattoo with the words proclaimed up on the Esplanade of Edinburgh Castle and then at the Mercat Cross in Edinburgh, declaring the Queen as sovereign and ending with the prophetic words 'to bless the Royal Princess Elizabeth II with long and happy years to reign over us.' As the Lord Lyon pronounced the words he could not have known that Her Majesty would go on to become the longest-reigning monarch in British history.

In May of 2002 I had been propelled into local politics as the Councillor for the town of Kelso where I live. The incumbent had died unexpectedly and, searching unsuccessfully for a candidate, I decided that the chance of being elected was so small there would be no harm in standing in the by-election. But I was elected, and when that happens it is too late to say 'I did not mean it'. You have to grit your teeth, smile and do it. So I came to the Tattoo that year with Council duties to carry out

The Edinburgh Military Tattoo celebrates

The Queen's Golden Jubilee 2002

EMT 2002 programme celebrating Her Majesty the Queen's Golden Jubilee.

during August as well.

I had asked the Royal Corps of Musicians from Tonga if they would play at the Border Union Show in Kelso at the end of July the day before the Tattoo production conference and Major Ve'ehala had agreed. The Tongans turned up at the show without their instruments when the airline carrying them said that it needed to fill its cargo hold before it would bring them. Undismayed, the Band delighted the crowd with their Polynesian dancing before it was suggested that the musicians – who were in the main big men – should take part in the tug of war against Peebles, the winners of the inter-rugby club competition. The two teams picked up the thick rope but as soon as the Tongans applied their weight to the rope, it snapped. It was not planned but it could not

The Royal Scots Dragoon Guards.

An ancient traditional Tongan Warrior dance to the rhythms of the Tongan Kailao.

A member of the Royal Corps of Musicians from Tonga shows how much the band can relax.

have pleased the crowd more.

For this rather special year, the Tattoo brought together acts from Australia, India, New Zealand and Tonga in the Commonwealth, from the former colonies in America and from one of the other European monarchies in the Netherlands to join the massed pipes and drums which were augmented by bands from Australia, Canada, New Zealand and South Africa and the military bands of the Royal Marines, the Scots Guards and the Royal Air Force. The Massed Pipes and Drums played for the first time a new tribute written for the Tattoo by Major Gavin Stoddart, MBE, BEM, Director of Army Bagpipe Music – the Golden Jubilee of Her Majesty Queen Elizabeth.

One thing that strikes visitors to the Netherlands is the large number of cyclists, which may not be surprising in a relatively flat country. There has been a Bicycle Corps in the Dutch Army since 1894 and a band on bicycles was first formed in 1917. It was disbanded in 1940 and reformed in 1995 as part of the Mounted Corps, which carries on the traditions of the Band of the Regiment of Cyclists

The Dutch Bicycle Band doing bicycle drill.

in the Royal Netherlands Army. The Netherlands had been ruled by Queens since 1890 and so it was fitting that Queen Beatrix, who had been on the throne since 1980, should have sent the bicycle band to celebrate this Golden Jubilee in Edinburgh.

The Esplanade of Edinburgh Castle is on a slope and I rather foolishly hoped aloud that our Dutch visitors would be able to stop before they reached the sea, but we need not have worried. The cyclists were not only perfectly in control but played and sang 'the Bicycle Song' and 'Tulips from Amsterdam', carried out dismounting and remounting exercises and, to the surprise and delight of the crowd, threw in some unexpected comedy as well. They returned later on foot with a Scottish medley before they burst into the Benny Goodman and Gene Krupa 1930s hit 'Sing, Sing, Sing'.

There are five monarchies in the Commonwealth other than the UK's own, and one of these is Tonga. The Polynesian state of 169 islands was ruled at the time of Her Majesty's accession by Queen Salote who became one of the most popular figures at the Coronation in 1953 with her cheerful smile and wave whilst travelling in an open carriage on that cold, wet day.

To have the Royal Corps of Musicians from Tonga at the 2002 Tattoo, therefore, was inspired and the most entertaining band, led by

A graceful Tau'olunga dancer from Tonga.

A dancer from the Indian state of Manipur.

Regiment (raised in the reign of Her Majesty's great, great grandmother Queen Victoria) and from New Zealand came the incomparable and energetic New Zealand Army Band. After their own displays, the three bands from the Southern Hemisphere combined before they all marched off to 'We Are the Boys from Way Down Under'.

From the north-eastern Indian state of Manipur came the Jawaharlal Nehru Manipur Dance Academy Company who combined the dynamic drum dances of the region with martial arts. The remote rural area had no standing army so every citizen – men and women alike – were expected to defend their land with sword and spear, and this part of the area's history was reflected in the colourful barefoot display.

Major the Honourable Ve'ehala, brought us their music from Polynesia ending with a tribute written by Queen Salote to mark the first official visit to Tonga by Queen Elizabeth II in 1953 – 'Nepitune'. To complete the 2002 honours we received a visit from Queen Salote's son, King Taufa'ahau Tupou IV, to take the salute.

Australia sent the band of the 10th/27th Battalion of the Royal South Australia

Even though the United States of America went its own way in 1776, for more than two centuries the country has maintained its special relationship with the United Kingdom which has grown ever stronger. The United States Marine Corps also has many ties and traditions which link them to Her Majesty's Royal Marines so it was a great pleasure to welcome their tribute from the Albany Band of the United States Marine Corps.

When many Scots emigrated they took their customs with them – including their Highland dancing – and the Edinburgh Tattoo Highland Ceilidh Dancers extended the hand of welcome to dancers bringing their skills back to Scotland from Australia, Canada, New Zealand and South Africa for the Jubilee and who formed the symbol E II R at the end.

At the Tattoo in Wellington in 2000, we heard the voice of a young New Zealander of Scottish and Maori descent, Joanna Heslop. She had come

The Household Cavalry.

The Tattoo Highland Dance Company.

to Edinburgh for the Golden Jubilee Tattoo and sang 'I Vow to Thee, My Country' and a beautiful love song from her native New Zealand, 'Pokare Kare Ana', composed about the time of the First World War and so popular in New Zealand that it is sometimes called the country's unofficial national anthem.

Then the Tattoo brought us back to reality with a reminder that soldiering is not only parading in smart uniforms but also taking on the country's hard tasks

such as, in this case, hunting down terrorists and arms smugglers. Brigadier Jameson had previously commanded Scotland's senior regiment and our only cavalry regiment, the SCOTS DG. They had just returned from their second tour of Kosovo, where their main task was to eliminate terrorism and arms smuggling, and the Regiment's Light Troop laid on a display of how efficiently they went about their business.

Earlier, the SCOTS DGS Mounted Troop of Greys and

the Regiment's magnificent Drum Horse, Ramillies, presented to them by Her Majesty the Queen in 1987 and carrying the Regimental Standard, were accompanied by the Pipes and Drums of the Scots Dragoon Guards and the Band of the Scots Guards. This would be Ramillies' last appearance at the Tattoo. He was retired after the show and died three months later.

Three weeks after her Coronation in 1953 the Queen and the Duke of Edinburgh came to Scotland and were drawn in state from the Palace of Holyroodhouse to St Giles Cathedral for a national service of rejoicing at which Her Majesty received the Honours of Scotland – the Scottish Crown Jewels.

The Tattoo recreated some of the pomp and splendour of that occasion by bringing the beautiful Scottish State Coach on to the Esplanade. It was built in 1830 and has had much care lavished upon it since. It bears on top a model of the Crown of Scotland and carries the Royal Arms of Scotland and the insignia of Scotland's highest decoration, the Order of the Thistle.

Within the coach were Scotland's ancient Honours: the Crown, the Sword and the Sceptre. These are the oldest sovereign regalia in the British

The Manipur dancers.

Isles, borne in procession through Edinburgh before the Queen on the visit following her coronation. Leading the Coach and the Honours was a detachment of the Life Guards. This was followed by the Blues and Royals and the mounted troop of the SCOTS, from Canada, members of the Royal Canadian Mounted Police and Lord Strathcona's Horse, and from India, riders from the President's Body Guard of the 61st Cavalry Regiment. It may not have been strictly historically accurate, but it made a magnificent spectacle in front of the old Castle as the Tattoo paid its tribute to the 50 years of Her Majesty's reign.

The Tattoo itself was memorable, but making it unique was the appearance of Her Majesty herself on Monday 5 August at the start of the first week.

Members of the audience who were fortunate enough to be there that evening saw the Queen arrive to be greeted by a Guard from the Highlanders and members of the Queen's Body Guard for Scotland – the Royal Company of Archers in their Border green tunics, their parade

bonnets surmounted by golden eagles' feathers and carrying their traditional longbows.

As Her Majesty made her way up the East Stand to the Royal Box, accompanied by His Royal Highness Prince Philip, Duke of Edinburgh, the Bands played an extract from Sir William Walton's Orb and Sceptre which was written as a processional march for Her Majesty's coronation in Westminster Abbey in June 1953. Knowing the acuity of her observation and her remarkable memory, the Queen will have noted how appropriate the music was to start her evening at the Tattoo.

2003
Elections for all the Councils in Scotland were held in May 2003 and, to my amazement, I had no opponents so I walked back in and once the dust had settled was elected as the Convener of the Council, the equivalent of a Mayor south of the border. The difference was that, south of the border, the post lasted for a year, but in Scotland it was for the full term, in this case four years. So I returned to the Tattoo as the elected Convener of Scottish Borders Council with those

duties to carry out as well.

Two weeks before the Tattoo began, I was loading a van in a farmyard at Stichill near Kelso to set off to sell butter, cheese, quiches and a host of other popular products at a farmers' market in Edinburgh when I broke my ankle. I had stepped on the edge of a concrete slab and heard a crack. The lady who owned the farm said firmly that it could not be broken, so we carried on.

We had a successful day at the market and on the way home stopped for a late lunch and then went to the Borders General Hospital, where a consultant surgeon said the ankle had indeed fractured, but that it was not too bad, and so gave me a tubigrip bandage and walking stick and sent me home to mend.

I like to be active at the Tattoo. At the rehearsals at Redford Barracks and at the Castle, I like to walk about getting to know the performers and picking up little pieces of information which I can store in my script in case they are needed. On the nights of the shows I climbed the stairs up to the microphone at the top of the East Stand several times a night; I walked up into the Castle to talk to the pipers and drummers and collect any little messages,

The pre-1801 Union Flag.

and talked to the people in the seats set aside for disabled people under the north stand and found out where they all came from before finally settling at the microphone for the show. In the 2003 stands there was no lift, so it had to be a slow climb up the stairs.

It is remarkable how quickly bones can mend and although I moved more carefully, especially on the wet cobblestones in the Castle, the episode was like the challenge ten years earlier of working in Aberdeen during the day and presenting the Tattoo at night: I found a way of managing and it had no effect on my voice and my ability to narrate the show.

In 2003, we marked the 400th anniversary of the Union of Crowns of Scotland and England in 1603, the raising of the Royal Scots in 1633 and the ending of the Korean War in 1953. We had already marked the Coronation the previous year so I gave it only a mention in its 50th anniversary year.

Edinburgh Castle was a particularly good setting to mark the Union of the Crowns, since King James VI of Scotland and I of England, the son of Mary Queen of Scots,

The pipers and drummers of the Black Watch just back from Iraq.

Korean warriors in their 8th century uniforms.

had been born there in 1566 and had already been King in Scotland for 36 years before he united the two thrones. He ruled for another 22 years and his reign of 57 years and 246 days was, then, the longest of any monarch in the British Isles. It was only surpassed by King George the Third in 1820, and then Queen Victoria in 1901, before the present Queen became our longest-reigning monarch in 2015.

The show opened as always with the massed pipes and drums, but after the main body had finished their first set, the audience cheered the pipes and drums of the Black Watch, who had just returned from service in Iraq and marched on in their desert combats playing 'Highland Laddie'.

In 1609 – six years after King James united the Crowns of Scotland and England and four years after he survived the assassination attempt of the Gunpowder Plot – the vessel *Sea Venture*, on its way to Virginia to relieve Jamestown (named after

Gombey dancers from Bermuda.

the King), was wrecked on the islands which became the colony of Bermuda. Nearly 400 years later, we were delighted to welcome the Band of the Bermuda Regiment to Edinburgh.

I was particularly pleased to see them as I had gone to Bermuda in 2001 with the Imps and had recommended that we should invite the Band and, more interestingly, the Island's unique fusion of African, Indian and European cultures in its Gombey dancers. These are masked and vividly costumed 'crowds' of dancers who turn out at holidays in Bermuda dancing frantically to loud, frenzied drumming in their all-encompassing costumes. The dancers wear tall conical head-dresses which sport ostrich feathers and cover their faces. These are reputed to be a throw-back to the time when the 'bondpeople' in Bermuda would 'relax' on Boxing Day and New Year's Day, the only days when they were not required to work, and the dancers would express their feelings about their conditions and, by covering their faces, do it anonymously.

It was King James VI's son, King Charles the First, who in 1633 gave Colonel John Hepburn a Royal Warrant to raise a regiment in Scotland for service in France. That Regiment became the Royal Scots which claims, from its antiquity, the honour of being the First of Foot and Right of the Line as the oldest infantry regiment in the British Army. It served from its inception until it was amalgamated with the King's Own Scottish Borderers into the Royal Scots Borderers on Tuesday 1 August 2006.

Because of their claim of antiquity, the French regiment of Picardy (the oldest in the

The Top Secret drummers from Switzerland.

French line) sneeringly called the Royal Scots 'Pontius Pilate's Bodyguard'. The French said they were even older, being descended from the ancient Scottish Archer Guard of the Kings of France. The Scots returned the sneer by pointing out that if they had been on duty at the Holy Sepulchre, the Saviour's Body would never have left it, implying (rather profanely) that Scottish soldiers would not have slept on duty, whereas the French obviously had.

Actors from the Scottish Community Drama Association helped to recreate some of the Regiment's early days while they were joined by members of the Regiment to relive some of its more recent glories.

The Korean War was remembered with the first appearance of the Traditional Band of the Army of the Republic of (South) Korea in its distinctively Asian uniforms dating back to the 8th century. The Band had dedicated its performance to the memory of all the United Kingdom's armed forces who fought for the Republic's freedom and I had the honour of reading a Korean *salpuri* for peace for departed souls as their graceful dancers glided across the Esplanade with their coloured fans. A *salpuri* is an

The Flying
Gunners of the
Royal Artillery.

ancient Korean rite designed
to wash away evil spirits.

This was also the year when
the Top Secret Drummers
from Switzerland made their
debut in Edinburgh. The
Swiss Top Secret Drum Corps
was formed in 1990 by seven
friends who wanted to develop
Basel-style drumming beyond
its traditional roots. They
went international ten years
later and reached Edinburgh
in 2003, where they were
immediately popular with
their juggling drumsticks and
spinning Swiss flags. They
have gone on being spectacular
crowd-pleasers with their
precision drumming and 17th-
century uniforms ever since.

The Flying Gunners of

the Royal Artillery Motor
Cycle Display Team provided
a speedy and noisy contrast
to the elegant turning of the
Tattoo's Highland Dancers,
who combined with the
Schiehallion Dancers from
Canada to perform a sword
dance of the Great Wheels.

One of Britain's oldest
allies is Oman, with links
stretching back to 1646 and
the East India Company.
So we added the musicians
of the Royal Army of the
Sultanate of Oman; the
pipers and drummers who
are always taught by Scots
and the dancers of the First
Band for Culture and Folklore
formed to conserve and teach
the traditional dances and

songs of the Sultanate. They presented a traditional dance in which the girls collected precious water, protected by their young warriors. The audience took a particular delight in the band's dancing piper, Lance Corporal Abdul Rahman Said, who showed just how adaptable the pipes could be in the right hands.

By contrast, the razor-sharp precision of the United States Army Drill Team was a true challenge to a narrator as well as to the members of the team. The Third United States Infantry (the Old Guard) created the US Army Drill Team in 1957 to maintain a heritage of service which has spanned two centuries. It has a unique dual mission as the Army's ceremonial unit in Washington DC, which includes serving as the official escort to the President of the United States and guarding

Traditional Omani dances.

The Tattoo Highland Dancers, joined by dancers from Canada.

the Tomb of the Unknown Soldier in Arlington National Cemetery and carrying the responsibility of protecting the capital during times of national emergency.

On the Esplanade of Edinburgh Castle, this team performed with the precision of a superbly engineered machine and I had to apply all my concentration each night to make sure that the narration of what they were doing had the same pinpoint accuracy. The members of the Drill Team carried 1903 Springfield Rifles fixed with a sharp, chrome-plated bayonet. These bayonets really were sharp and had injured members in rehearsals,

so I had to ask the audience not to take flash photographs in order to allow the men absolute concentration and avoid them being distracted at a critical moment. They carried through their routine without orders, including the final, daring front-to-rear overhead rifle toss. Although it did not happen at this Tattoo, a high wind in an open-air arena such as Edinburgh Castle is a serious hazard for such a manoeuvre.

With the Massed Bands of the Royal Artillery, the Royal Logistic Corps and the Adjutant General's Corps the Tattoo managed to add two teams from the Kings

Highland dancing on the Esplanade.

Troop Royal Horse Artillery. The 13-pounder guns and limbers of the RHA had all seen action in the Great War and they were a tight fit on the confined space of the Esplanade, but the teams handled the challenge superbly, unhitching the guns and leaving them on the Esplanade before the horses left. The troop was named the King's Troop by the Queen's father, King George VI, after he had visited them in 1947 and the Queen allowed them to retain the name in his memory. The guns which the teams left behind were fired during the finale music of 'The Conquest of Paradise', so it was only sensible to ask the children in the audience to hold the hands of any nervous parents.

2004

The great invasion of Europe on D-Day had taken place 60 years before the 2004 Tattoo, so the first tune played by the Massed Pipes and Drums at the start of the show was 'The Sixth of June 1944'. Brigadier Jameson also introduced that year a lead service which would revolve each three years between the Royal Navy, the Army and the Royal Air Force. The youngest service, the Royal Air Force, took the lead in this first year so the Tattoo audiences were treated to a flypast each night by a Tornado or a Jaguar, a Hawk, a Nimrod, a Typhoon or a Tucano. These aircraft could provoke some distress in local pets but they were enjoyed by the audiences.

They gave me as the narrator a fine discipline each night to get the warm-up finished before the aircraft arrived above the Esplanade. I could not see them coming as they approached up the line of the Royal Mile behind me, but RAF pilots are superb at arriving overhead precisely on time. Speaking up to but not overlapping with the 'pips' of the time signal was a daily challenge which every radio announcer on the BBC had to master. Beside me at the Tattoo I had a small portable clock which I set to the exact time each night using the Speaking Clock and, following the count down, I could carry the warm-up right up to the moment the plane appeared. The people around me never quite grasped how it was done and tried to be really helpful by giving me countdowns

Dancers from the Indian state of Mizoram, dancing the Cheraw.

either verbally or with their fingers, all of which I had to tune out while I read the script and watched the clock.

In 2002, we had watched the dancers and martial artists from Manipur in North East India. Two years later, we welcomed the Mizo from Mizoram state to the south of Manipur. For 2,000 years the Mizo had celebrated success with colourful dances which are not community dances. Their most colourful and popular dance, Cheraw, is only performed by a few girls with exceptional skills, usually to celebrate events such as a bumper harvest or a marriage ceremony. The young men sit face-to-face on the ground tapping long pairs of bamboo poles together while the girls dance in and out of the opening and closing poles to the rhythm of gongs, a small drum and, in Edinburgh, a military band. Wearing their traditional handwoven costumes, the girls have to be exceptionally nimble to avoid being trapped by the closing poles that move to the inexorable rhythm of the music – and there was not an evening when any of them were caught.

Because this was an RAF year, we were treated to the precision of the Queen's Colour Squadron of the RAF carrying out the movements of the services drill book without a word of command and to the music of the pipes and drums and the RAF bands. The RAF also had a strong influence on the Highland Dancers from the Tattoo team, by then sponsored by a producer of natural water, and the Australian Ozscot Highland Dancers to celebrate the Royal Air Force and the Royal Australian Air Force with circling propellers and their familiar red, white and blue roundels in a dance they called *Wings*.

In the past we had welcomed Zulu dancers from South Africa but this year we heard a band unlike any other military band in the world, with African drums, banjos and marimbas added to the usual instruments of the South African Navy Band, led by a former Grenadier Guards Bandsman Commander Mike Oldham. Celebrating the tenth year of the country's new democracy, the audiences loved the addition of the marimbas, the exuberant alto sax playing of Warrant Officer Willi van Sale and the singing of Leading Seamen Nombali Mkhize and Emmanuel Twala.

On the other side of the world, the Baltic state of Estonia had re-emerged as an independent nation in Europe in 1990 and the world-class Aesthetic Gymnastics Group Club Piruett was formed. In 2004, they came to the United Kingdom for the first time and to the Edinburgh Tattoo where they amazed the audiences with their fluid, dynamic movements to the music from the film *Gladiator*.

To remind us that this was an RAF year, the RAF Squadronaires turned back to the heady days of the Second World War when the Royal Air Force Dance Orchestra attracted the cream of London's top bands. The Squadronaires was re-formed

Gymnasts from Club Piruett, Estonia.

in 1987 to continue the great traditions of its predecessors, so we just had to hear Glenn Miller's 'In the Mood'. The RAF Massed Bands also used his 'Chattanooga Choo Choo' and Ron Goodwin's marvellous film music for *633 Squadron*.

From the far side of the world, for the first time in Edinburgh, came the precise formality of the Military Band of the People's Liberation Army of China with its skilled musicians and female dancers, all attired in red and white uniforms, who gave an exhibition of beautifully drilled and intricate marching.

It was inevitable that some group wanting to gain publicity for its political stance against the Chinese treatment of Tibet would try to use the Tattoo to give themselves a platform. They wrote to the Producer and were given space in the Lawnmarket to unfurl their banners but that was not enough. Believing that they were smarter than the police and the Tattoo organisers, some of them bought tickets for the show one night. I watched them fumbling with a banner, upside down as it happened, when the Chinese appeared on the Esplanade but the group never did get its banner unfurled or the right way up. They were swiftly removed by the police and missed the rest of the show

They chose the wrong place to promote their cause. Some 17 years earlier, I had been asking pointed questions in the European Parliament about the Chinese behaviour in Tibet and had even hosted His Holiness the Dalai Lama in a highly successful visit to the Parliament to make a speech about the Chinese treatment of his homeland. I am certain, however, that it was quite wrong to try to use the Tattoo to promote a political cause in this way. The Tattoo has never espoused a political cause and I hope that it never will.

The incident, which was so efficiently carried out that it was hardly noticed, had a rather comic sequel when a few nights later another spectator in a different part of the stands tried to unfurl a perfectly innocent banner wishing someone a Happy Birthday and had his view of the show curtailed with an equal lack of ceremony.

2005
The Tattoo was off down under again in 2005 to Canberra for Australia Day and then on to Sydney with a Salute to Australia, but I shall return to those in Act Nine.

Back in Edinburgh in August, we gathered for a Royal Navy year to celebrate 60 years since the end of the Second World War and 200 years since the Battle of Trafalgar.

We welcomed back old friends in the Imps motor cycle display team, the Trinidad and Tobago Defence Force Steel Orchestra and Drums, the Russian Cossack State Dance company and His Majesty the King of Norway's Guard on the 100th anniversary of its formation.

The Band and Bugles of the Light Division delighted the crowd with their unusual fast marching at 140 paces to the minute and their accelerando when they start slowly and work up to their fast pace playing 'Zorba the Greek' which always takes a trick.

The Highland dancers wore the new Highland Spring tartan and they were joined by

Fireworks on the roof of the Aussie stadium in Sydney.

the New Zealand Highland dancers in a display which saluted the Royal Navy of Admiral Lord Nelson with their version of the many tasks needed to sail a fighting ship of the line, finishing in the form of a White Ensign.

Her Majesty's Royal Marines were summoned again to deal with a ruthless group of heavily armed anarchists who stole the Scottish Crown Jewels from the castle and demanded a ransom for their safe return. You may remember that a group tried to steal the same Crown Jewels in 1997 and were thwarted, then, by Royal Marines from the Comacchio Group. This time, the Marines, with recent successful operations in Sierra Leone, the Balkans, Afghanistan and Iraq behind them, made short work of the thieves to the cheers of the audience.

But it was not only the fighting Marines who were on deck. There were three Royal Marines Bands from Scotland, Plymouth and the Royal Naval College who

84

carried us back 200 years for the highlight of the Tattoo from the year 1805, when the Royal Navy fought one of the most decisive of all sea battles.

Only the British Fleet stood between Britain and Napoleon Bonaparte, and the Royal Marine Bands and the dancers fought again a musical version of Admiral Lord Nelson's great victory at the Battle of Trafalgar against the backdrop of a capstan and poop deck on the Esplanade with images of the British and French vessels projected on to the Castle walls. Once again it was a nice challenge for the narrator to tell the story of the lead up and the battle at the right moments in the music and keep the audience riveted.

2006

Her Majesty turned 80 in 2006 and her daughter, the Princess Royal, agreed to become Patron of the Tattoo.

To mark these events and the bringing together of old Scottish regiments in the new five Regular and two TA battalion 'super-regiment' of the Royal Regiment of Scotland, we presented a tribute to the Scottish Soldier. Right from

the opening 'Fanfare for the Scottish Soldier – the Gathering' the programme built steadily through its guests from around the world towards the story of Scottish heroism on the battlefield.

This was a happy theme for me, for unexpectedly in this year I was back in uniform again, having been appointed as Honorary Colonel of the Lothian and Borders Battalion of the Army Cadet Force. It made a nice change to do the Tattoo wearing my old Parachute Regiment maroon mess kit with its shiny new Colonel's insignia and sporting my old red beret as I walked up into the Castle to talk to the pipers and drummers and chat to the crowd.

After the Massed Pipes and Drums had opened the Tattoo as they always do, we heard the charming voices of the Watoto Children's Choir from Uganda. These are boys and girls who have lost one or both parents to AIDS or some other tragedy and who tour the world with a message of hope for Africa's children.

The mountain warriors of Nepal – the Gurkhas – have been keeping the peace with the British Army since 1816

Watoto singers from Uganda.

and over the years they have developed a special association with the Scottish Regiments born out of mutual regard for courage, hardihood and honour. The Band and the Pipes and Drums of the Brigade of Gurkhas played familiar music in their own distinctive style, including Zorba the Greek, before marching swiftly away to the Brigade of Gurkhas March 'Yo Nepali'.

The Highland Dancers were joined by dancers from South Africa to remind the audience that dancing was a very old practice of Scottish soldiers and the New Zealand Army

Band left everyone breathless with the energy they put into their innovative performance.

The ancient practice of Kung Fu is not just a martial art, but a strict code of physical and mental discipline and we welcomed 60 students from the Jiangxi Xishan International School in China which has a wide reputation for the quality of its Kung Fu teaching. This was the first time the audience had seen this art at the Tattoo, complete with its own form of highly controlled energy and red flags.

Performers from South America had been missing from the history of the

The boundlessly
energetic
New Zealand
Army Band.

Tattoo so we were intrigued and thrilled to welcome to Edinburgh the Concert Band of the Army of Chile. Each August, Chileans celebrate the anniversary of the birth of their 'Liberator' and first head of state General Bernardo O'Higgins, who wrested the country from Spain in 1810 with the help of the Scottish Admiral Lord Thomas Cochrane.

The band marched on to the Esplanade playing the marvellous 'Radetsky March' and using its traditional stiff-legged Gran Parada step, which is rather better known as the goose step. The Chilean Army was the first country outside Europe to adopt the goose step, importing the tradition from Prussian

military drill after the War of the Pacific of 1879–1883

With the Band came the Evendart Artistic Company of dancers in spectacular Spanish-style costumes dancing the Cueca, the Chilean national dance. Two of the ladies in wide skirts were showing the Chilean national flag, the country's coat of arms and the Sausau

Jiangxi Xishan kung fu fighters.

from the Chilean possession of Easter Island. This was another act which needed little slivers of narration to explain the significance of what the band, the singers and the dancers were doing, and was just one of the small tasks which make the job so fascinating.

I enjoyed explaining the red plumes worn by the band as they played the March of the Red Hackles, 'Penachos Rojos', but I do not think the Black Watch (which wears its own red hackles) has taken up the music. I thought it was helpful to explain that the tune 'Adiós al Séptimo de Línea' was a tribute those who

fought in the Pacific War of 1879–1883 and that the Band

formed the name 'Chile' ready to sing the 'Obertura Patriótica Chilena' before they marched away to 'We're No Awa' Tae Bide Awa''. Afterwards the Band presented me with a clock set in an attractive mottled stone in the shape of South America with Chile picked out in a blue stone.

I did not need to say a word about the second visit by the Top Secret drummers from Basel in Switzerland, their spectacular drumming spoke loudly for itself.

Then we honoured the very long traditions of Scottish soldiers. The bands of the Scots Guards, formed in 1642 by King Charles I, and

THE GREATEST SHOW ON EARTH

the Coldstream Guards, the modern descendants of the soldiers of General George Monck's New Model Army who marched south from the Scottish Border town of Coldstream to restore Charles II to the throne in 1660, marched on playing a tune from the South African War, 'Soldiers of the Queen'. From there, we told the story of the role of Scottish soldiers throughout British and European history.

Before there was a British Army, Scottish soldiers had fought in conflicts across the continent of Europe. They learned their trade in the fighting between the clans in the Highlands and the raids across the border with England and were sought after at home and abroad by monarchs with battles to fight. Scottish archers formed the bodyguard of the Kings of France, the Garde Ecossais, as a result of the Auld Alliance with the French. But it was not until the 17th century that the forerunners of the regiments which gave Scots such a high reputation on the battlefield were formed.

The Tattoo covered their roles on the British mainland, the European continent, India and North America. We honoured their gallantry and skill as peacekeepers for the United Nations and NATO after the two world wars and in the many other places where British soldiers have been asked to go since: Korea and Suez and the Far East; Aden, Central America and Northern Ireland; the Falklands, the Balkans, the Gulf and Afghanistan.

Men in the uniforms and the transport of previous conflicts, including horses, helped to bring the music and the story to life. Superb projections of pictures of some of the battles and famous figures of conflicts covering more than four centuries, along with the cap badges of the regiments we were honouring, added to a fine and moving cavalcade to remember the old Regiments in the year when the new Royal Regiment of Scotland was formed.

We ended the 2006 Tattoo by bidding farewell to the Producer who had steered the mighty show to huge worldwide and commercial success, Brigadier Melville Jameson.

I have only appeared on the

Esplanade once and this was a couple of nights before his last show, on Thursday 24 August, when I introduced Mel, the Lord Provost Councillor Lesley Hinds, the General Commanding the Army in Scotland Major General Euan Loudon and the man who would make a special presentation to Mel, Sir Sean Connery, who handed over a silver model of Edinburgh Castle to Mel's especial delight.

Two nights later, as the final show neared its close, Mel, a former commander of the Royal Scots Dragoon Guards, was carried on to the Esplanade on one of his regiment's smaller armoured vehicles, a Combat

Dancer with the Chilean national flag on her skirt.

THE GREATEST SHOW ON EARTH

The Cueca, with dancers from Chile.

Vehicle Reconnaissance (Tracked) or CVR(T).

The pipes and drums of the Royal Scots Dragoon Guards circled the vehicle carrying the Producer, who had been the Pipe President of the Regiment when the combination of its military band and pipes and drums burst into the hit parade. In 1972 they knocked chart toppers T Rex, Alice Cooper, Donny Osmond and the New Seekers off the top spot with their recording of 'Amazing Grace' and stayed at the top for six extraordinary weeks.

So the Massed Bands of the Coldstream and Scots Guards, the Royal Regiment of Scotland, the Brigade of Gurkhas and, from overseas, the New Zealand Army Band, the Army Band from Chile, plus 13 pipe bands played 'Amazing Grace' and 'Auld Lang Syne' before they all marched away, leaving Mel to circle the Esplanade on the CVR(T) to receive the cheers of the crowd as he left the historic 'showground' for the last time as Producer.

2007–10
Major-General Euan Loudon

A NEW YEAR began with a new Producer, but not a new face. Into the breach had stepped Major General Euan Loudon CBE who had been the General Officer Commanding 2nd Division and Governor of Edinburgh Castle from 2004 until he retired from the Army in early 2007. Euan had served with the Royal Highland Fusiliers, commanding its First Battalion before he soldiered in the Gulf War in 1991, earning an OBE. He moved on to serve in Northern Ireland before returning to Scotland.

It was also the year when Her Majesty the Queen and His Royal Highness the Prince Philip, Duke of Edinburgh, celebrated their Golden Wedding Anniversary. So this was a natural event to mark with the usual flair of the Tattoo on the Esplanade of Edinburgh Castle within its theme of the excellence of British military music in the same year as the Royal Military School of Music celebrated its 150th anniversary.

Performers came from around the world to tip their musical hats to the Royal couple. From nine time zones away on the other side of the world came the delightful young ladies of the Taipei First Girls Senior High School Band & Drill Team from Bei Yi Nyu, one of the most prestigious girls' schools in Taiwan. The school's most challenging activity is its percussion marching band, honour guards and colour guards and we were delighted to welcome them all to Edinburgh. These schoolgirls were awestruck by everything they saw and wanted me to autograph just about everything they possessed. I still treasure the intricate 'love-knot' they gave me before they left.

British military music grew from drums thundering out orders on the battlefield to the magnificent sight and sound we know today. The drums were initially joined by fifes and we had one of the foremost groups recreating that traditional sound – the Middlesex County Volunteers Fifes & Drums from the Boston area of the United States, which I had first seen at Springfield, Massachusetts, in 1995. Wearing the uniforms of the American War for Independence in the late 18th century, the team gave the big audiences another immaculate demonstration of American precision in their music and movement.

The Tattoo Highland Spring dancers were joined by dancers from Australia, Canada, New Zealand and South Africa in order to celebrate the Diamond Jubilee with an exuberant dance to the Appalachian Roundup.

The irrepressible Imps from East London came back with their remarkable motorcycle display skills including high speed cross-overs, riding on top of a ladder, small and large pyramids, and a heart-stopping jump over not only a car, but the rest of the team as well, before the six-year-old mascot Slavi Antanasov gave the salute for the whole team.

Then came three superb demonstrations of just how adaptable and versatile military music can be.

The Band of the Moscow Military Conservatoire, conducted by Lieutenant Colonel Igor Tsupikov, was established in Moscow in 1935 as a school for military conductors. Each of its members contributes a very Russian passion to its brilliant interpretations of great Russian composers.

The very British Blues and Royals trace their origins back to the restoration of King Charles II in 1661. The Royal Horse Guards and The Royal Dragoons, which were formed from the disbanded cavalry of Oliver Cromwell's New Model Army, came together in 1969 to create a regiment with a mounted band which had nearly 350 years of musical history behind it.

Military music may sound the same to many people, but there is one military band which could only come from the home of steel band music Trinidad and Tobago. In 2007 the Trinidad and Tobago Defence Force Steel Orchestra and Drums brought with them Limbo dancers Pte Donna Lee Lewis and Pte Nyron James to demonstrate a super-human agility under the repeatedly lowered and, eventually, burning bar. The effect left the big audiences breathless with amazement at their strength and nerve. The only sad part of the band's joyful performance was the final appearance at the Tattoo of Drum Major WO1 Rufus Lewis, who had led the band out from its first appearance at the Tattoo ten years earlier.

Then, with musical illustrations from the Royal Artillery State Band, the band of the Royal Regiment of Scotland and the Light Cavalry

Band (who marched on to 'Arnhem', the tune written to commemorate the greatest battle of Airborne Forces during the Second World War), I enjoyed telling the long story of military music from the days of orders being beaten out on drums on European battlefields up to the 21st century.

In Scotland, military music began with pipers leading the ancient Scottish clans into battle. Then influences came from further east and we heard a small 17th-century band, headed by a Turkish 'Janissary' with his Jingling Johnny, which marched on playing the popular Royalist ballad from the 17th-century

Pte Donna Lee Lewis limbo dancing under a flaming bar.

THE GREATEST SHOW ON EARTH

Civil War 'When the King Enjoys His Own Again', which the Jacobites borrowed for their 1745 rebellion.

The band added further instruments, first the fife, then 'hautboys' – early oboes – and bassoons to play the tunes the soldiers were singing. Then they showed how musicians entertained soldiers off the battlefield but more importantly helped them on it, encouraging troops with rousing music and treating the wounded inside the infantry squares typically used at the Duke of Wellington's heroic victory at the Battle of Waterloo.

By the middle of the 19th century, military bands were quite independent of each other and played as they thought best. But matters came to a most embarrassing head in 1854 in the Crimea on Queen Victoria's birthday when all the bands came together and played 'God Save the Queen' in different arrangements and in different keys. The result was so awful that the Queen's cousin, the Duke of Cambridge, the Commander in Chief, decided to have all the bands trained to the same standard and in

1857 he founded the Royal Military School of Music – Kneller Hall – to train bandmasters and bandsmen for the British Army.

The role of bandsmen in the 20th century was illustrated by the heroism of Bandsman Thomas Rendle of the Duke of Cornwall's Light Infantry, who was awarded a Victoria Cross for carrying his wounded colleagues to safety under sustained shell and rifle fire as a medical assistant. That was followed by the Second World War morale-lifting music of Glenn Miller and Dame Vera Lynn and the contemporary music played in the Falklands, the Gulf, Iraq and Afghanistan.

The whole item showed that the role of bands today is as important as it ever was, providing musical support not only to our troops but also to the great events of state and such national celebrations as Her Majesty's Diamond Wedding anniversary.

Scouts have been helping at the Tattoo, principally as programme sellers, since the first show so it was only right that Scouts, Explorer Scouts and Leaders from around Scotland should join the cast at the finale each night to celebrate the centenary of the World Scout Movement with the enduring finale song from the old Scout Gang Shows 'Crest of a Wave'.

Before the show on Wednesday 15 August the Lord Provost of the City of Edinburgh, Councillor George Grubb, presented the prestigious Queen's Award for Enterprise in International Trade to The Edinburgh Military Tattoo for more than doubling its export earnings over three years. He handed the award, in the form of a splendid Queen's Award crystal bowl, to Mrs Susan Lawton, who had then been working for the Tattoo Company for 26 years and headed the highly successful box office and who is now the head of all the Tattoo's sales.

In May, I had been re-elected as Convener of Scottish Borders Council, which was quite fun when I came down after the show and saw my fellow Lord Provosts, Provosts or Conveners as guests on Tattoo nights.

2008

Volunteers have guarded our shores for centuries and were formalised as the Territorial Army in 1908 by the Scottish lawyer, philosopher and politician Richard Burdon Haldane, so it was natural that we should pay our respects to those men and women who give up so much time and skill to serve this country on their centenary in the 2008 Tattoo. It was also the centenary of Scotland's only school offering education to the children of soldiers serving with the Scottish Regiments and Battalions, Queen Victoria School in Dunblane. Opened in 1908 it was Scotland's memorial to the Scottish soldiers and sailors killed in the Boer Wars in South Africa.

The massed pipes and drums played tunes which commemorated some of the actions in which Territorial soldiers have fought alongside Regular forces with courage and distinction, including The Heroes of St Valery, The Bloody Fields of Flanders and El Alamein.

Once again, Major General Loudon had drawn an entertaining group of performers from around

The Lochiel Marching Team from Wellington, New Zealand.

to Scotland to toast these centenaries. After their first appearance in 1999, we welcomed back the Golden Eagles from the Southeast Missouri State University and the Holland School of Visual and Performing Arts built on the banks of the mighty Mississippi River in America. They brought with them another scintillating display of marching, playing and dancing, along with their twirler Whitney Beusink.

The mighty Mississippi stretches from the Gulf of Mexico nearly to the Canadian border and the Edinburgh Military Tattoo Highland Spring dancers traced the 18th-century emigration from Scotland first, to Nova Scotia, and then right across the vastness of Canada. To tell the story, the dancers were joined by the Canadiana Celtic Dancers to weave those historic links and their effect on Canadian culture.

The Singapore Police Force Band had not been to Edinburgh since 1991, the year before I took up the microphone, so I was intrigued to see them for the first time. They brought with them the Women's Police Pipes & Drums Platoon and the Gurkha pipes and drums. It carried us around to the far side of the world with their musical impression of the cultural diversity of their eastern nation and the creative harmony of its many races with the remarkably athletic and colourful symbol of the Lion.

After the colourful chaos of the lion dance, we headed south to New Zealand where many Scots had emigrated and had a profound influence on the culture there. The audience was once again delighted to welcome the glamour and precision of the 27-time New Zealand champion marchers in the Lochiel Marching Team. They had first come to Edinburgh in 1978, again in 1983, 1993 and 1997 and were back for a fifth and immediately popular visit. There have been lasting matches made between Lochiel ladies and other performers over the years that they have been at the Tattoo and I expect there will be more over the years to come.

The first performers from India appeared in Edinburgh in 1962, then not for another 40 years until 2002. More had come in the following two years and in 2008 we cemented India's long association with Britain with the first visit of the Indian Army Chief's Military Band.

Rather like the Lochiels, His Majesty the King of Norway's Guard gave us another remarkable display of precision marching and playing adding a nice touch mixing the very Scottish Loch Lomond with their signature Old Ranger March as they left the Esplanade.

Then it was the chance for the dancers of Queen Victoria School, backed by their pipers and drummers and flanked by the school's colour party, to show off their Highland dancing skills in this centenary year. The youngsters from the Dunblane school are always a spectacular sight in their scarlet jackets and Hunting Stewart tartan.

The combined bands of Her Majesty's Royal Marines from Scotland, Plymouth and Portsmouth poured down the Esplanade to 'A Life on the Ocean Wave' before breaking into an unmistakeably Royal Marines programme, culminating in a dramatic playing of the Perthshire-based composer Dougie McLean's 'The Gael' from the film *The Last of the Mohicans*.

The Lone Piper played a fitting 'Centenary Toast' as our final tribute to the men and women of the Territorial Army in their centenary year.

Halfway through the Tattoo's run, on the morning of Friday 15 August we had all gathered at Edinburgh Zoo for a special ceremony when His Majesty King Harald of Norway had asked us to elevate the special penguin, which the King's Guard had adopted in 1972, on his behalf. After various greetings which included a message from the King read by Nils Egelien, the officer from whom the penguin had drawn his first name, I had the honour of reading the King's citation.

HARALD THE FIFTH by the Grace of God of the country of Norway and Our Realms & Territories King, Head of the Country and Defender of the Faith, to Our Trusted and Well-beloved, Nils Olav, Commander in Chief of His Majesty's Loyal Guard GREETINGS. FORASMUCH as We taking in to Our Royal Consideration that the Place and Office of Peerage of Our Realm be bestowed upon you on this day the fifteenth day of August Two thousand and eight, and is Our Gift and Disposition and We being well satisfied with loyalty, courage and good endowments of Our Trusty and Well-beloved Nils Olav, and reposing entire trust and confidence in you as a Penguin in every way qualified to receive the honour and dignity of Knighthood and the Office aforesaid.

The penguin waddled forward and was knighted in the King's name by Major General Euan Loudon, the Tattoo Producer, and the King's Guard Trumpeters blew a fanfare. The next time you go to Edinburgh Zoo look out for a special penguin and be ready to call him Sir.

2009

2009 proved to be a busier year than usual with four extra, smaller, Taste of the Tattoo events added to the schedule.

These were designed to be the Tattoo's contribution to what was billed as the 'Homecoming Celebration', which was intended to attract people of Scottish ancestry to visit the country. The year was appropriately selected, as it was the 250th anniversary of the birth of the poet Robert Burns. Scotland's culture and heritage was one of the themes of the year and the Tattoo was perfectly designed to fit that.

Adding these extra events was testing for the performers, for although these extra shows were during the day, two in

Stilt-walking
Chinese dancers
from Shaanxi
Province.

the first week and one in each
of the following weeks, they
all had to return to Edinburgh
after each one and prepare
for the full show at night.

At night on the Esplanade,
Homecoming remained
the theme and our visiting
performers gave the visitors
in the audience a spectacle
to take home with them.

The Royal Corps of
Musicians from Tonga
had prepared an especially
colourful display of Tongan
and European music advancing

to the sound of a Kelea, a
special seashell blown to warn
of the approach of an enemy in
the huge Polynesian war canoes
called Kalia. Happily, this
canoe was friendly and quickly
transformed itself into a St
Andrew's Cross accompanied
by a Scottish Dance to
Scotland the Brave which
became a Tongan War Dance
to the sound of Polynesian
drumming. But for me, the
highlight of every Tongan
performance was the most
elegant Tau'olunga dancing

of the ladies from the Tongan forces, whose expressive hand movements said far more than words could manage.

From the South Pacific, the Tattoo elegantly mixed contemporary military music and action from Europe with its tribute to Robert Burns and a glimpse of ancient Chinese culture. Robert Burns was serenaded by four young singers from the Royal Scottish Academy of Music and Drama – Elysia Leech, Lynda McMinn and brothers Christopher and Douglas Nairne – with three of Burns' best loved songs 'Ye Banks and Braes of Bonnie Doon', 'Green Grow the Rashes O' and 'Ae Fond Kiss'. During this, they were joined by the choir of the Calgary Burns Club from Canada.

Later, the Tattoo Highland Dancers with the Ozscot Dancers from Australia recreated Burns' classic tale of the dangers of falling prey to the supernatural after taking too much to drink in the 18th-century tale of Tam o' Shanter.

The audience was jerked back to the 21st century with a realistic demonstration of how the medical teams of the Royal Air Force worked in a combat zone to help friend and foe alike in evacuating casualties in Afghanistan. The aim was to give the wounded the best care possible by bringing a helicopter-borne tactical Accident and Emergency department to them on the battlefield.

It was a fast-moving four-minute display of how courageous the pilots were flying into a hostile area to treat and remove casualties as fast as possible. A brilliant example of how well the Tattoo's developing projection worked was the simulation of the tailgate of a Chinook helicopter superimposed on the drawbridge and entrance to the Castle.

I watched this demonstration, adding carefully placed prompts to keep the audience informed of exactly what was happening on the ground, not realising that the following year a young relative, Sergeant Simon Harmer, operating as a Combat Medical Technician on patrol in Afghanistan, would be rescued after an IED blast by just such a team as had been demonstrated at the Tattoo. When I heard the grim news that he had lost his legs in the blast I could picture immediately the superb process by which the British forces extracted him and flew him straight back to the UK, where he has made an inspiring recovery.

A wholly different view of the world through the natural turning of the seasons in the Chinese province of Shaanxi followed with the ancient Chinese rural festival of She Huo, which is performed to celebrate the end of winter and the coming of spring. The ceremony prayed for good weather for the crops, a bumper harvest, a prosperous State and peaceful people. Opening with Chinese trumpets and continuing with Chinese music, the ceremony brought to Edinburgh terracotta warriors, stilt walking as though riding on long-legged bamboo horses, flower garlanded poles and ancient battleship dances. The performers from Shaanxi were fabulously arrayed in the most glorious and colourful costumes as their contribution to our Homecoming.

Most of the people in the military forces of Switzerland are conscripts. As a result, The Swiss Army Central

Band can draw on first-class musicians who have become superb musical ambassadors for their country. Most people think of Switzerland as a country of mountains; to pitch sounds from mountainside to mountainside and across deep valleys, the Swiss developed the art of yodelling and the extraordinary alphorn with its very long stem and wide bell end. So the band had to finish with a demonstration of its yodelling skills before the deep vibrations of the alphorn were played alongside it.

At one time these fairly simple instruments were prohibited under sentence of death in places where Swiss mercenary soldiers were employed because the sound caused them to break down in tears, desert or die. Happily, there were no such casualties at the 2008 Tattoo. Alphorns and yodelling are not the only music at which the Swiss are skilled. Their drumming is famous around the world and the Top Secret Drummers returned for the third time with their distinctive development of the Basel style of drumming.

2009 was a Royal Air Force year so the Central Band of

the RAF, the Bands of the RAF College and the RAF Regiment along with the RAF's salon orchestra were joined by the other bands on parade. Flight Lieutenant Matt Little sang Going Home before the two young ladies from the RSAMD sang Amazing Grace as the finale piece.

And we were honoured by another Royal guest from Tonga with the visit of His Majesty King George Tupou VI, whose father had taken the salute in 2002.

2010

2010 was a special year when The Edinburgh Military Tattoo became The Royal Edinburgh Military Tattoo, with the title bestowed by Her Majesty the Queen.

The first time I used the new title, however, was not in front of Edinburgh Castle but in the Sydney Football Stadium where we first celebrated our Diamond Jubilee with 60 Years of Valour, Mateship and Glory to sell-out crowds on our second visit to the 'sunburned country'. But I shall say a little more about that in Act 9.

In Edinburgh in August, we celebrated not only our Diamond Jubilee but also noted the 150th Anniversaries of the Cadet movement in the United Kingdom and the Army Physical Training Corps, the 125th of the Soldiers, Sailors, Airmen and Families Association, the Centenaries of Army Bagpipe Teaching, the Girl Guides and the death of Florence Nightingale. There were far too many to manage within the show, but I was able to mention them all at the beginning of my warm-up each evening.

As I said at the start of the Diamond Jubilee Royal Edinburgh Military Tattoo, 'In the last 60 years, we have welcomed many popular performers from around the world, but none have been more popular than the magnificent sight and sound of the Massed Pipes and Drums.'

For this Tattoo we had gathered the players of 19 and 40 Regiments Royal Artillery, the Royal Scots Dragoon Guards, the Royal Dragoon Guards, The Queen's Royal Hussars, First Royal Tank Regiment, the Black Watch Third Battalion, the Royal Regiment of Scotland and staff and students from the Army School of Bagpipe Music and Highland Drumming.

In 2010, the Tattoo became Royal.

From overseas came the South African Irish Regiment, the South Australia Police pipes and drums, the Swiss Highlanders and the Citadel from South Carolina in the United States of America. They played many old favourite tunes and marched away to an old Scots tune 'Happy We've Been A' Thegither' and the new tune 'The Royal Edinburgh Military Tattoo', by the new Director of Army Bagpipe Music and Highland Drumming, Captain Steven Small. The pipes and drums always generate one of the loudest cheers every night as they emerge from the Castle, spilling over the drawbridge on to the Esplanade, bringing the colour and spectacle of their tartans and the sparkle from their buckles and buttons in the powerful lights.

In what was to prove his final Tattoo, Euan Loudon had assembled a cast of great variety from different corners of the world displaying a bewildering range of skills.

One of the many blessings of the collapse of the Iron Curtain between East and Western Europe has been the availability of performers from Eastern Europe, whom we had not been able to welcome before. So we were particularly happy to see and hear for the first time the Representative Band of the Border Guard from Poland. It had been 70 years since Polish forces arrived in Scotland after the fall of France during the Second World War. Many Polish soldiers settled in Scotland after the War and the links remain strong.

This Polish Band was unique in using the traditional folk instruments from the mountains of southern Poland and the drum major carried as his mace a traditional, ornamental mountaineer's axe called a *ciupaga*. The band's instruments included Shepherds' bells called *zbyrcoki* and *trombity beskidzkie* which were similar to alphorns. The musicians brought us a great deal of Polish music which had not been heard at the Tattoo, before they marched away to seal the longstanding friendship between Scotland and Poland with that great old tune which has had many titles over the years but which most folk know best as the 'Road to the Isles'.

As the Poles marched away, five-year-old Joe Dennis rode over the drawbridge on his

50cc motorbike, leading out another tightly controlled display by the Imps motorcycle display team of youngsters ranging in age from five up to 16 from East London. This was the team's 40th year and as always they produced a bewildering display of tricks on their 50, 70 and 230 cc motorbikes. There were two, three and four way crossovers. The four way crossover is known as the St Andrews Cross and for good measure the senior riders aged between 12 and 16 showed that they could do it just as well riding in reverse as going forwards. There were tricks with such names as Gone to Sleep, Double Side Saddle, Mini pyramid with L plates, Flower, Flying Angel, the Fountain, the Backwards Ladder and the Jimmy. All performers bore the cap badge symbol of the Royal Signals which started the idea of service motor-cycle displays with their White Helmets team. Jimmy was merely a corruption of the name of the Italian sculptor Giambologna, whose original figure of the winged messenger of the gods Mercury is in the Pitti Palace in Florence. The Motorcycle and Sidecar

always drew hearty laughs as nine-year-old Adam Murray steered around the Esplanade at an angle with five-year-old Joe Dennis firing a giant water pistol towards the crowd.

No self-respecting motor cycle display team would be complete without a pyramid. The senior members on five bikes with 17 riders, commanded on different nights by the Captain 16-year-old Lee Lucas and Vice Captain Kieran Fevrier, carried out this difficult manoeuvre with skill every night with Wayne Scott (aged 13) carrying the Union Jack on top. I doubt if the big audiences really appreciated how supple the linkmen between the bikes had to be to keep the whole stack together.

Representing the United States of America we welcomed back, after a break of 19 years, the young musicians from the Regimental Band of the Citadel, the Military College of South Carolina. With the Band came the Citadel's Pipes and Drums. In 1981 The Citadel adopted its own tartan with the colours carefully chosen to symbolise the traditions of the Citadel – the college colours of blue and white, gold representing the brass on cadet uniforms and red symbolising a cadet officer's sash.

The Band of the Brigade of Gurkhas brought cheers from the crowd, as it always does, with a short programme starting with a traditional Alap played on a Nepalese flute. The Band then moved into its classic accelerando of 'Zorba the Greek', starting slowly and working steadily up to its familiar marching pace of 140 paces to the minute and marched briskly off to the Regimental March 'Yo Nepali'.

Although the Highland dancers had been increasingly moving towards displays of contemporary Highland dancing, in this Diamond Jubilee year the Tattoo Kinloch Anderson dancers, joined by New Zealand Highland dancers, started by celebrating 60 years of Highland dancing at the Edinburgh Tattoo. They paid their tribute to the first Producer, Lieutenant Colonel George Malcolm, and the first Director, Lieutenant Colonel Alasdair Maclean, who were the only two officers in the Army up to professional standard as Highland dancers. Two military dancers and a solo

piper led the display before the New Zealanders danced on to form a Saltire followed by the Scots in ceilidh mode.

Then the sound of the exotic Middle East floated from the battlements of the Castle as the Jordanian *rababa* echoed into the night. The *rababa* is probably the oldest string instrument, dating at least as far back as the eighth century, and is almost certainly the direct ancestor of the European violin. For this Tattoo, it ushered on to the Esplanade the first visit of the Jordanian Armed Forces Contingent since 1963.

The members of the Bani Hashem Honour Guard on horseback, which hails from Jordan's numerous Bedouin tribes and have an honoured role in Jordan's history, circled the Esplanade. The Jordanians are referred to as the people of the red *kouffiyah*, a reference to the red and white head dress still common throughout the country and worn by the Pipers and Drummers, who marched on playing Atholl Highlanders and Jordanian Kouffiyah, followed by the band playing the march 'Glorious Victory'.

King Abdullah II encouraged the formation of a drill team in

2007. It was the most recent addition within the Honour Guard which also contains the mounted Honour Guard and the Circassian Honour Guard wearing the distinctive black *tsey*. The Circassian Honour Guard has had the duty of ensuring the personal security of Jordan's monarchs, starting in 1921 with King Abdullah the 1st. The guard continues to serve Jordan's reigning monarch, His Majesty King Abdullah the 2nd, in a largely ceremonial role.

The combat skills and knowledge of desert terrain of the Bedouin were instrumental in the Great Arab Revolt against the Ottoman Empire in 1916 and after the success of the Arab Revolt the Bedouins formed the core of the Arab Legion, the forerunner of the Jordan Armed Forces. As a reminder of that turbulent period and as the Jordanians marched off to 'The Army Song', there were displayed at the top of the Esplanade replicas of two of the Rolls Royce vehicles converted for military use in the First World War and used in the Great Arab revolt. They had been specially flown to Edinburgh for the Tattoo at the request of King Abdullah II, who honoured us by taking the salute on Wednesday 18 August.

Displays of straightforward gymnastics are pretty rare on Tattoos, but in 2010, the Army Physical Training Corps, which was formed in 1860, decided it would show its modern skills operating everywhere the Army serves, both in peace and conflict, delivering physical and adventurous training, sport and rehabilitation to all Army personnel. To commemorate its 150th anniversary, the Corps had resurrected a show which incorporated speed, strength, skill, stamina and suppleness which, combined with teamwork, represented the qualities that the Corps aims to develop in all soldiers. The High Horse Display Team, helped over the horse by a combined band from the Grenadier and Coldstream Guards conducted by Major Kevin Roberts, was a reminder of just how versatile they could be moving, diving and rolling at dazzling speed. Eight of the instructors had completed six-month operational tours in Afghanistan within the previous year. The hazard

of such a display in the open air is rain, but there was only one night when the weather made the display too dangerous to complete fully.

The energetic New Zealand Army Band hardly gave the audience time to get its collective breath back as the super-fit musicians raced through their always entertaining programme before marching away behind the mace of their Drum Major Staff Sergeant Philip Johnston. As well as Drum Major, he was a tuba player of world renown who had won the national tuba solo 15 times and the champion of champions twice.

I think it is fair to say that no matter how good and how entertaining other bands are, there is no sound in the world quite like the sound of the British Guards Bands and to Edinburgh in its Golden Jubilee year came the Band of the Grenadier Guards, celebrating its 325th anniversary, and the Band of Coldstream Guards, a mere 225 years old, who marched on together playing

THE GREATEST SHOW ON EARTH

Soldiers of the Queen. As they broke into 'You Raise Me Up' a patrol from the Coldstream Guards Corps of Drums, who had served in Afghanistan earlier in the year, crossed the Esplanade to demonstrate some of the humanitarian work which bandsmen are called on to do. In this case, it was ensuring an Afghan family had been able to move forward safely, as part of the Army's work to rebuild the country.

John Barry's 'John Dunbar Theme' from the film *Dances with Wolves* had been transformed in recent years into a tribute to the British troops in action. As the finale, the Massed Bands conducted by the Tattoo's Senior Director of Music, Lieutenant Col Graham Jones MBE, played with the stirring singing of two Icelandic students from the Royal Scottish Academy of Music and Drama, Bjartmar Sigurdsson and Jakob Höltze. They sang the moving 'Here's to the Heroes'.

And to emphasise that British troops were facing danger every day and every night in Afghanistan, the Tattoo's Guard of Honour was found from The Third Battalion Rifles who had just returned from a tough seven-month deployment in the Sangin District of Helmand province.

The Tattoo had evolved subtly over the years from being a display of military talents to a musical show which was selling out every night. It had adapted, and must continue to adapt, to continue its remarkable place in global entertainment. The show was becoming a serious diplomatic asset to the United Kingdom as well as to Scotland, and it was about to take a giant step towards becoming one of the finest examples of 'soft power' on the planet.

2011 to the Present
Brigadier David Allfrey

WHEN THE 2010 Tattoo ended we had no inkling that it would be the final Tattoo under Major General Euan Loudon, but on 7 September, ten days after the Tattoo had folded its tents for another year, he resigned. We were all shocked at the news and sorry to see him go, but thankfully, it was nothing to do with the Tattoo. He had been a professional golfer before he joined the Army and had been offered the job of Chief Executive of the St Andrews Links Trust, a dream job for him as he said later. So the Board had the unenviable task of searching for another Producer with less than a year to prepare for the next Tattoo.

It is not possible to explain quite how it does it, but the Army usually manages to produce the right man for the hour and so it was that by the turn of the year a veritable dynamo of energy, Brigadier David Allfrey MBE, a former

Commander of the Royal Scots Dragoon Guards and 51 Brigade based in Stirling, became the next Producer.

Some of us had seen him in action when he created The Pipers' Trail in 2008 to celebrate the centenary of the Territorial Army. For this, a group of pipers on a six-week trail was formed to walk to and perform in towns and cities the length and breadth of Scotland, starting in Shetland and finishing in Edinburgh.

The Tattoo had a new Producer, the spectators had new stands, and I had a new title. I was no longer the narrator, but henceforth I would be the storyteller. It was a good signpost to the way the shows would be constructed in future years.

More or less from the start of my association with the Tattoo I had heard complaints from people that the seats were a little tight for them and they felt squashed by their neighbours. (It never seemed to occur to people that it was the spectators who had become a little too broad for the seats.) However, the old stands had served the Tattoo well for 36 years and I am sure that we had squeezed far more than their value out of them, so we moved into the 21st century with a £16 million collaboration. This increased the size of the seats by 35 per cent, offered much more space and better access for disabled spectators, more spacious production rooms, bigger hospitality areas and rather less time needed to erect and dismantle the new stands.

Once again, there were far more anniversaries than we had time to cover in the show, the 500th anniversary of the Royal Military Police; the 400th anniversary of the Society of High Constables of Edinburgh; the 150th Anniversary of the One O'Clock Gun and the 90th anniversary of the Royal British Legion Scotland. But this was a Royal Navy year, so our theme was the sea and ships.

David Allfrey has never been a man to feel bound by what has gone before, so he immediately changed the opening of the Tattoo to show the Lone Piper of the night on the Esplanade greeting the Salute Taker of the night with a toast in Scottish Gaelic and a dram of whisky from a *quaich* – a traditional, shallow Scottish drinking cup with two straight handles or *lugs*. Tradition requires that after a toast has been drunk from a Quaich it is turned upside down and the drinker kisses the underside to show that he has drunk every drop.

The toast the pipers had to learn was:

Ceud mile failte dhuibh
uile gu baile Dhun Eideann
agus chun a' Chaisteil.
Moran laithean sona
dhuibh is sith.
Slainte do'n Bhanrigh!
Slainte dhuibh uile!

Which roughly translated means:

One hundred thousand
welcomes to you all to
the city of Edinburgh
and to the Castle.
A long happy life and
peace to you all.
Health to the Queen!
Health to you all!

The Dutch Bicycle Band in WW1 uniforms head downhill on the Esplanade.

I had the toast with a phonetic rendering of the Gaelic ready in case the piper should dry up during the toast, but no piper ever has and my Gaelic has remained unused.

With the audience comfortably seated in the new stands it was only natural that the 2011 Tattoo should start with a salute to the stands. This involved a van driving on to the Esplanade to let the Royal Marine drummers out, who were dressed in boiler suits and hard hats as 'workmen'. Dressed as such, they took up work on the stands by raining hammer blows on metal pieces, which naturally led into a rhythm picked up drummers in the stands, trumpeters on the Castle ramparts and the bands on the Esplanade.

I do not know how many of the audience were fooled by the start, but they seemed to enjoy something different which led into something familiar. The Massed Pipes and Drums, whose set was filled with familiar tunes, ended with a new tune composed by Captain Steven Small, the Director of Army Bagpipe Music, 'The New Stand'.

This was a Royal Navy year, so it was not surprising that those great seafarers, the Dutch, should have provided one of the star acts of the night – although on bicycles, not on boats. The Music Corps of the Bicycle Regiment of the Royal Netherlands Army had been a huge success in 2002 and returned with the Band on 32 bicycles singing 'the Bicycle Song' and a good deal of humour mixed in with their music, which had to include 'Tulips from Amsterdam'. There was a mock puncture and pump routine and an accident which saw the bicycle carried off on a stretcher while the player was left on the ground before the whole equipage departed down the sloping Esplanade to the strains of Loch Lomond.

The Scots are not always good at remembering their heroes, but the first visit of the Brazilian Marine Corps Martial Band with its bagpipes was a dig in the ribs to remember that the first commander of the Brazilian Navy in 1822 was Admiral Thomas Cochrane from landlocked Lanarkshire, christened the Sea Wolf by the French and rewarded by the Brazilians with the title of Marquess of Maranhão.

Of course, the Brazilians came with their infectious samba rhythm and their special occasion red uniform jackets. The characteristic white ribbon cap has become a tradition since it was introduced into the Brazilian Marine Corps in 1890 by the former Scots Naval Battalion Commandant, Lieutenant Arthur Thompson.

Over the years during which the British Empire was being created, thousands of vessels bringing raw materials to Britain and carrying our goods out to the world sailed the oceans, protected by the guns of the Royal Navy. The firepower of a Royal Navy 18-pounder gun was formidable – a cannon shot could punch through three feet of solid oak and had a range of a mile and a half. Many of the guns came from the Scottish Carron Iron Works, most famously the short-barrelled carronades, which lasted well into the 19th century.

On the Esplanade, Scotland's oldest ship, representing the sailing navy, now berthed in Dundee. The 1824 46-gun frigate HMS *Unicorn* had been recreated and crews demonstrated 18th-century gun drills with embers from a previous shot being swabbed out, the gunpowder rammed home and followed by a cannon ball. This was followed by the hard work of running out the gun on its carriage, which could weigh over two tons, in a rolling ship before it could be fired at just the right moment.

In the second half of the 19th century, the Royal Navy fought only one ship to ship action, but its Naval Brigades of seamen and Royal Marines were trained in land warfare and fought in actions as far apart as China and Africa. When the security of the South African trade route was threatened in the Boer War, the action of a Naval Brigade dragging its specially adapted guns overland to relieve the Siege of Ladysmith in 1899 went down in history as the origin of the famous Naval Gun Run.

And each night, teams from different naval bases strove against each other in a competition which was a spectacular test of strength, discipline and team work in order to show the 'Gunners' Ethos' of challenging the individual to strive for their limits and then beyond. In the first week, HMS *Sea Hawk* from Culdrose in Cornwall took on HMS *Heron*, based at Yeovilton. In the second week, HMS *Raleigh* from Plymouth challenged HMS *Neptune* from Faslane in the West of Scotland and in the final week, the sailors from HMS *Sultan* at Gosport raced the team from HMS *Collingwood* in Fareham.

I urged the crowd on to cheer for the team nearest to them as the crews exchanged 100 lbs limber wheels on the 1200 lbs guns. They then fired three rounds, turned, exchanged wheels again and fired another three rounds before the guns were rejoined to their limbers and the teams raced uphill to the finish. It was fun, and making sure I got the team right on each side was important in order to keep up the momentum

Celebrating the fishing heritage of Scotland.

THE GREATEST SHOW ON EARTH

right to the last tired stride.

I was intrigued and pleased to discover that, when the Royal Navy wanted to test its members to their limits, it sent them not to sea, but to the mountains of Bavaria in southern Germany to pit themselves against the elements there with the challenge of really tough adventure training. So, after a break of 25 years, it was appropriate that we should welcome from that rugged Bavarian terrain, the German Mountain Army Band from Garmisch-Partenkirchen, with its distinctive sound of the Bavarian mountains. For the third year in a row at the Tattoo, alphorns were played on the Esplanade as the Bavarian Band played an Alpine Horn Concerto on three of the long instruments. Then woodchips flew on the Esplanade as some of the musicians engaged in rhythmic log chopping with their axes swinging to the rhythm of the band.

And the Bavarians were immediately followed by a splendid display of synchronised woodchip brushing by members of the Arena Team from the

Royal Highland Fusiliers Second Battalion, The Royal Regiment of Scotland. They were followed by The Royal Edinburgh Military Tattoo Highland Dancers and West Ulster's Total Dance Group, which celebrated the lives of the fisherfolk of Scotland and their silver harvest. They explained in dance movements the rhythm of the sea, its tides, its moods and its fish, before the Dutch musicians dismounted from their bicycles, captured the many complex moods of the oceans in a programme of superb, stirring music.

After the music, the Navy was back in action with Royal

Members of the Bavarian band chopping logs in time to the music.

The life of
Scotland's fishing
communities
celebrated
in dance.

Marines to demonstrate
how they could swiftly
and effectively subdue and
overcome pirates at sea
and the show finished with
the finale suite from *How
to Train Your Dragon*.

But it was a not a dragon
which marched down with the
Guard of Honour but the then
mascot of the Royal Regiment
of Scotland, the Shetland pony
Lance Corporal Cruachan
III and his Pony Major
Corporal William Perrie.

For a narrator, this
was a busy and rewarding
Tattoo. There were a great
many interjections and
commentary for all of the
action items as well as
during some of the music to
keep the audience aware of
what was going on, often at
speed, on the Esplanade.

In one of his moments of
quiet contemplation after a
rehearsal for the 2011 Tattoo,
David Allfrey had been
sitting in one of the stands
on his own, as he thought.
He was disturbed by the
sound of feet and, looking
along the stand, he saw a fox
looking back at him. They
regarded each other for a
few moments before the fox
licked a front paw and trotted
away on more important
business. The encounter
was to bear a different
fruit the following year.

2012

David Allfrey began to
demonstrate his global vision
for the Tattoo in February
of 2012, when the Tattoo's
Patron, the Princess Royal,
was the Guest of Honour at
a dinner in the Edinburgh
International Conference
Centre, to thank the people
who were willing to be the
Tattoo's Ambassadors. David
had a powerful belief in
the force for good that the
Tattoo represented around the
world, projecting Scotland,
principally, but also the

Edinburgh schoolchildren become Pictish warriors.

United Kingdom and the value of her Armed Forces.

I had the honour of narrating the evening's entertainment, which was, in effect, a mini-tattoo. The Band of Her Majesty's Royal Marines Scotland, the harpist and composer Phamie Gow and The Royal Edinburgh Military Tattoo Highland Dancers danced to the piping of Corporal Neil McNaughton, from the Army School of Bagpipe Music & Highland Drumming. And of course, there were speeches from the Chief Executive of the Edinburgh International Conference Centre and the Tattoo Producer before Her Royal Highness took her leave.

I treasure the memory of that evening and keep a picture of it as my screensaver.

2012 marked the 60th anniversary of Her Majesty's accession to the throne. She was now the second-longest-reigning monarch and the Tattoo celebrated with something of the long history of the land over which her reign stretched.

Youngsters from the Erskine Stewarts Melville Schools opened the tattoo with a *carnyx*, a large Iron Age Celtic trumpet-like instrument and some 40 diminutive 'Pictish' warriors percolating down through the Audience to form up on the Esplanade. After three 'fanfares' on the *carnyx*

who joined the dancers from
Scots College in Sydney to
portray the weaving of tweed.
Youngsters from Erskine
Stewarts Melville School
and the Lyceum Theatre sat
among standing stones to
become the avid listeners to
musical tales of great heroes
and heroines. Meanwhile, the
Highland dancers with the
Canadiana dancers celebrated
the distilling of whisky.

The tri-service Australian
Defence Force Band came to
represent the Commonwealth,
of which her Majesty is the
head, fast forwarding from the
arrival of the tall ships in the
18th century to the modern
country of the 21st century
with the music of the Scottish
Australian group AC/DC.

Then, in one of the most
imaginative scenes any tattoo
audience will have seen, the
OzScot Highland Dancers
created the flowing movement
of Scotland's move into the
Industrial Revolution and
the long Scottish pedigree
in heavy engineering using
iron and steel to create
engineering marvels in ships
and bridges and railways
around the world. Soldiers
dressed as steel workers added
welding sparks using large

and the roar of a modern
jet fighter, a Pictish shaman
cast his diamond bright
spell over the audience to
transform the old stones into
a place of wonder in order
to celebrate the history of
our land and 60 years of Her
Majesty's long reign. It was a
dramatically different opening
and set the new Producer's
mark on how different the
Tattoo was going to be with
his imagination and flair.

The thread of how
Scotland's earlier people
had coaxed a living from
the soil was taken up by the
pipers and drummers and
the young Highland dancers
from Queen Victoria School,

props at the four corners of the Esplanade in a colourful recreation of a foundry tempering and hammering hot steel, culminating in the Castle being covered in projected boiler plate.

Youngsters of any age have always loved cartoon comic strip characters and the United States Naval Forces Europe Band from Naples, in Italy, recreated the music of many of the best-loved of the fantasy characters – Popeye, Banana Man, Spiderman, Batman, Superman – who have delighted us in this century and the last. Through their ranks rode two of Scotland's favourite cartoon characters, Dennis the Menace and Minnie the Minx, brought to life by Brad McNicol and Joanna Dudgeon from Transgression Park in Edinburgh on BMX bikes. Brad demonstrated night after night just how remarkable and inventive BMX riders can be as he made his bike do tricks I am sure its designer never dreamed it could achieve.

The Top Secret Drum Corps from Basel returned in their black and white uniforms to demonstrate Scotland's willingness to adapt to the digital age and Silicon Glen and the King of Norway's Guard returned to tug us back to the Golden Jubilee of Her Majesty, remembering that His Majesty King Harald V had paid two visits to Scotland in 1994 and 2005. I remembered the first visit well. As one of the members of the Royal Company of Archers on duty inside the Palace of Holyroodhouse on the first day of the state visit, I had a wonderful position at the top of the stairs as Her Majesty and King Harald walked up after their drive through Edinburgh in an open carriage.

Then the Tattoo made a sweeping bow to the Coronation of Her Majesty as the climax of the 2012 show. The Bands of Her Majesty's Royal Marines Scotland, the

Dennis the Menace and Minnie the Minx.

Royal Regiment of Scotland, the Queens Division, Kings Division and the Royal Air Force Regiment played Royal Salute and tunes representing all parts of the United Kingdom before the Bands from Australia, Norway and the United States added their international weight to the occasion.

I had done a lot of research, including a trip to Westminster Abbey, to make sure I knew exactly the form of the Coronation service. Although my description was brief, it wasted no words in the description of the most important elements of the ceremony, with superb projections on the Castle walls as the combined bands played Sir Hubert Parry's 'I Was Glad' including Vivat Regina from the cast, George Frederick Handel's 'Zadoc the Priest', 'Crown Imperial' by Sir William Walton and 'Rule Britannia'.

But even after the magnificence of the scene and the music, the Producer had one more little trick up his sleeve. I asked the audience to celebrate Her Majesty's 60 glorious years of devoted service to this country and the Commonwealth by turning on thousands of diamonds of light from their mobile phones, cameras, torches or whatever they had with them to shine out from every seat as the bands played 'Diamonds are Forever'.

I certainly had not wanted to be a Councillor forever. When I was elected in 2002 I had told myself I would do no more than ten years. As it happened, the second full term was extended to five years to separate Council elections from the elections for the Scottish Parliament, so the poll fell neatly at the end of ten years and I happily took off the chain I had had made for the Convener in 2007 and handed it on. I thought it would give me a little more time and so it did – but only to start doing more than ever.

2013

In the autumn of 2012, David Allfrey told me the story of his encounter with the fox, believing that it would make a good little children's book. He said he would have to look for a writer who could tell the story and, without thinking of the consequences, I said that I wrote stories as well as scripts and I would be happy to do it.

For a couple of months, I tried opening after opening and nothing seemed to flow, and by the beginning of February 2013, I was at the point of admitting that I had bitten off more than I could chew and that I had let David down. At this point, however, I felt my backbone stiffening and I told myself that the members of my Regiment, the Parachute Regiment, did not give up but saw a job through to success. So I started again with new energy and in only a matter of days had drafted 12 stories about a little fox who had walked to Edinburgh from the Borders and had settled down on the Castle Rock.

Without a published book in hand, the Tattoo had arranged for the book to be part of the Edinburgh International Book Festival. A publisher saw it in the Festival programme and offered to take it on and at great speed an editor and an illustrator were found and brought my rough ideas to a finished book in time for the Festival and the 2013 Tattoo. Happily, children liked it and two years later it even won the Heart of Hawick Children's Book award for first

books. I liked that, because it was chosen by a vote of primary school children from the Borders where I live.

It was a good year to publish, as that was the year of Natural Scotland which became the theme of that year's Tattoo. Once again, David's vivid imagination saw the show start with The Big Bang. There was a huge explosion and a blinding flash from the castle as the youngsters from Erskine Stewarts Melville School and the Lyceum Youth Theatre poured over the Castle drawbridge like lava from the volcano from which Edinburgh Castle Rock was formed.

David ingeniously linked the growth of a plant from a

Alasdair Hutton shares his first book, *The Tattoo Fox*, with children from Erskine Stewart's Melville.

Schoolchildren pouring out of the Castle as lava.

single cell to the growth of a piper's Piobaireachd from a single note to its full flowering as the Massed Pipes and Drums. The Tattoo ceilidh dancers created the dawn of a new day and the dancers and musicians from the Ministry of National Defence Traditional Band from the Republic of Korea used cherry blossoms to mark the arrival of spring.

A placid fisherman was interrupted by the buzzing of the insect-like motorcycle

Imps imitating midges with all their amazing tricks. I was amused that although the Captain of the team was only 15, he insisted on my saying he was 16 so that he could appear older among the young ladies of the Tattoo dancers.

The Compañia De Danza Folklorica Tenochtitlan and the Monumental Jaguares Marching Band from Mexico created an Aztec dance of Life and Death before they bathed the Esplanade in the light and colour of a Latin American summer fiesta.

The irrepressible New Zealand Army Band represented autumn, bringing their gloriously fluid act right up to date by donning sunglasses and performing the extraordinary Korean hit 'Gangnam Style' between a Haka and some Vivaldi before the Lochiel Marching Team from Wellington represented the coming of night. The Orchestra of the Mongolian Armed Forces brought winter with a remarkable throat singer and a Khaanic legend portrayed by the troupe's extraordinarily supple dancers to show that a quiver of arrows becomes stronger when it is bound together.

The Bands of the Irish Guards, the Royal Logistic Corps and The Rifles celebrated the wildlife of Scotland from field mice to wildcats, from the salmon to the mighty stag and all the birds and insects in the air around us were projected on the Castle walls. Then we were delighted and privileged to have the remarkable life-sized 'puppet' of Joey the 'Warhorse' from the London stage production appearing on the Esplanade for the first two weeks of the Tattoo. I had seen the puppet when I was presenting the Household Division's Beating Retreat on Horseguards Parade in London and travelled down to ask the National Theatre if Joey would come north for the Tattoo. He already had too many commitments to manage the whole run, but he delighted the big audiences who did see him and the skilful puppeteers who brought him to life.

Of course, it was only natural that we would use music from Mars, Saturn and Jupiter in Gustav Holst's *Planets Suite* to accompany the fireworks at the end of each performance.

Since 2011, the Tattoo had appointed an artist in residence from among the students at Edinburgh's College of Art and in 2013, Danielle Callaghan's designs were projected on to the old stones of Edinburgh Castle to emphasise the theme of Natural Scotland. Projection has added enormously to the appeal of the Tattoo, with often elaborate pictures and designs illustrating and enhancing the acts as they brought colour and movement to the ancient Castle walls.

I was told by the shop in the Castle that sales of my little book about the Tattoo Fox always went up when people saw the huge image of the Fox projected on to the Castle.

2014

2014 was another Year of Homecoming, so the Tattoo theme of *Our Home, Friends and Family* was designed to welcome the thousands of visitors from across the world to Edinburgh and to the Tattoo.

It was also the centenary of the start of the First World War and on the first Monday of the Tattoo, 4 August, the date on which in 1914 Britain declared war on Germany, the audience was given little, battery-powered LED candles. I asked them to switch on their candles just before the National Anthem and to leave them on until 11.00pm, the hour at which the declaration of war became effective, when they could turn them off on their way home and reflect on the gravity of war and the sacrifices of the men who had marched away 100 years earlier.

To illustrate the Homecoming theme, the Tattoo followed the adventurous journeys made by many Scots as they travelled out to every corner of the globe, sent off with the majestic sound of the

Above and right: Zulu dancers from South Africa.

THE GREATEST SHOW ON EARTH

Massed Pipes and Drums ringing in their ears. Dancers wrapped in shawls waved off the emigrants on the way to their first stop in the George Cross island of Malta, from which we welcomed the Band of the Armed Forces of Malta and the Ellipsis Dancers who skilfully wove a Maltese Cross through the Band.

We followed the early voyages round South Africa pausing to welcome the iNgobamakhosi Zulu Dance Troupe with some of the battle songs from the KwaZulu-Natal iButho. The energy of the dancers was again a powerful reminder of just how fearsome were these remarkable warriors. The troupe's name was taken from the Zulu warriors who overcame the British at Isandlwana in 1879. I am sure that many in the audience admired the fortitude of the dancers, men and women, who danced with such undimmed energy unclothed from the waist up on cold and occasionally damp nights.

After South Africa we looked north to remember home and for the first time welcomed the Hjaltibonhoga Fiddlers from Shetland where once the Scandinavian earls from Norway had ruled until the 15th century and where to this day the Pretty Dancers – the Northern Lights – blaze across the night sky.

During the Second World

The Ellipsis Dancers create a Maltese Cross.

The Hjaltibonhoga Fiddlers from Shetland.

Dancers from
the Nagaland
Hornbill Festival.

War, Indian troops helped to turn back enemy forces in the North East of the country, where the names of Kohima and Imphal are written into the history books with honour. So it was a special honour to welcome from the Indian hill country of Nagaland, where Kohima is the capital, the Nagaland Folklore Group with some of the songs and dances from their annual Hornbill Festival. Every night, first to the apprehension and then delight of the audience, the leading Naga warrior dashed up the stairs at the front of the East stand and presented a traditional Naga spear to the Guest of Honour. I treasure the handsomely decorated *stole* with which the Group presented me, quietly, at the end of the Tattoo as a reminder of these marvellous, isolated people.

Morgan Bamford, the reigning adult World Champion Highland Dancer, led the Tattoo Highland dancers in a nostalgic glance towards home in The Gael. We then found ourselves fascinated by the precision and formality of Singapore, founded as a trading post by Sir Stamford Raffles in 1819 with the encouragement of two far-seeing Scotsmen, Philip Dundas and Lord Minto, and now one of the world's major commercial hubs.

They were followed by a

Maori warriors.

remarkable fusion of Maori and Scottish dancing from the Te Waka Huia and Te Whanau a Apanui Maori Kapa Haka Dancers and the New Zealand Highland dancers. I am not certain if this had been done before, but it worked beautifully to illustrate the arrival of the Scottish settlers in New Zealand and their integration with the Maori people there.

Any description of travellers to and from Britain would have been incomplete without the Caribbean and we were warmed again by the sunny performance of the Trinidad and Tobago Defence Force Steel Orchestra and Drums. This time they brought with them popular characters from their Spring Carnival, Damlorraine in which slaves exaggeratedly mimicked French fashions, the Fancy Sailor with his unsteady walk, another character in one of the many costumes worn at Carnival and the Moko Jumbe, a character on stilts who was derived from

Maori singer.

an African God, elevated to see danger ahead and looked on as the protector of a village.

Then, to remind the audience of a more serious side to the work of the military and to mark the 350th anniversary year of the Royal Marines, a squad gave a swift and decisive demonstration of how they would deal with terrorist infiltrators. The massed bands of the Royal Marines from Plymouth, Portsmouth and Scotland played a nautical set including a hornpipe which brought out the dancers again in sailors' costumes.

I knew that David Allfrey had been looking for a really good tune to bring on the cast and I was delighted when he accepted 'All Night Hooley on Glebe Street', which I had heard played at some of the brass band contests I introduced when I was not at the Tattoo. It was composed by a good friend and prolific and tremendously talented Scottish composer Alan Fernie. Both Alan and his delightful wife Brenda with their daughter Rebecca were able to come to the Tattoo and hear the music being played by a seriously big band.

Then, to welcome all the

The Home, Friends & Family programme, 2014.

exiles home again, David did something almost unthinkable: he encouraged the cast to let their hair down on the Esplanade with a 100-year party. In the 1960s, members of the audience came on to the Esplanade and jived. With the very big casts which the Tattoo now had, that was impractical, but the dancers were able to shake loose to such music as 'The Charleston', 'Rock Around the Clock', 'Is This the Way to Amarillo' and Pharrell Williams' 'Happy' with Michael Jackson's 'Thriller' along the way. That thrilled the audience, who made their appreciation of the whole performance, as well as that tune, particularly loud and vocal.

And after all that, Mark Knopfler's 'Going Home'

THE GREATEST SHOW ON EARTH

from the film *Local Hero* seemed just right to round off the homecoming Tattoo.

While the Tattoo was underway, my second little book of adventures, *The Tattoo Fox Makes New Friends*, which chimed with the theme of friendship, was published. The Fox and Castle Cat had inadvertently been taken back to Rosyth by the Band of the Royal Marines and the book started with their adventures as they made their way back to the Castle and found many new places to explore and new animals to meet around Edinburgh. I had written it during the winter when things were a little quieter after the Burns Supper season and now it was out in the bookshops and happily giving some new cheer to children.

2015

2015 was an ambitious year in which the Producer aimed to bring East and West together in his global concept of the power of the Tattoo to span such gaps.

After the opening fanfare 'East Meets West', the massed pipes and drums formed the yin and yang symbol, which in Chinese philosophy means that contrary forces are, in reality, complementary and interdependent in the natural world. They then gave way to the pipers and drummers of the Brigade of Gurkhas, celebrating 200 years with the British Army.

We swung to the west from where the United States Air Force Honor Guard Drill Team gave the sell-out audiences another sparkling display of precise weapon handling. These displays are always an exciting challenge for the narrator, who has to master the elements of the performance and learn precisely when to interject little explanations of what was happening.

Zulu warriors getting to grips with *The Tattoo Fox Makes New Friends*.

Thankfully, I had the invaluable help of Technical Sergeant Maurice Chaney, the team's Sergeant Major, who came up to my little box every night and made sure I was precise in the timing of each description. There were little, subtle signals as well, of which the audience was unaware, but on nights when the M-1 Garand rifles and bayonets became clammy or slippery, the team would march out without gloves and I knew that they would have to drop one of their more risky manoeuvres.

Although the young drill team members make it look easy, there are dangerous elements which it would be unwise to take lightly. The commander's final march down between two rows of spinning rifles and bayonets has to be timed precisely. The rifles weigh in excess of 13 lbs and the bayonets are very sharp. If the commander gets the timing of the walk down wrong, he or she could be badly hurt. On those nights when Technical Sergeant Chaney took command of the performance, the usual commander, Captain Cahn Wadhams, would come up and the show went on without a hitch. Coming up to help me gave Technical Sergeant Chaney a great view of the team's performance and I noticed that he was counting the beats of the actions, as the

One of the Shetland fiddlers.

team must have been counting in their heads. He was noting tiny imperfections which I could not see and of which I am sure the audience was unaware so that he could iron them out the next day. I had suggested that the team try the horse riding gloves with slightly pimply palms which I had found effective in gripping wet reins, but these did not give the sensitivity which the team members needed to feel the rifles during their complicated manoeuvres.

The Hjaltibonhoga Fiddlers brought more of the music of Shetland to the Scottish mainland before the theme swung east again and they joined in the Oscar-winning theme song of the 2008 film *Slum Dog Millionaire*, 'Jai Ho', which very roughly means 'let there be victory'. With them were the Tattoo dancers and the RAF Bluebells, three young lady singers dressed in RAF tartan saris, the band of the Royal Regiment of Scotland and the choir from Erskine Stewarts Melville Junior School.

The colour and movement of Bollywood comes to Edinburgh.

Boy meets girl among the Bollywood dancers.

That gave way to contemporary and traditional Chinese music from the band of the People's Liberation Army from China, thankfully without anyone trying to use the Tattoo as another excuse to make a political protest. We then saw an extraordinary creation of an old dragon legend from the Chinese province of Changxing. The dancers from Changxing gave a remarkable performance, weaving a dragon across the Esplanade, dividing it and creating lotus flowers from the scales.

We went west then to make way for the nearly 200-year-old traditions of duty, honour and respect embodied in The Citadel Military College from Charleston, South Carolina, whose young musicians with their band and the pipes and drums brought a variety of music. This included the old Irish march 'Killaloe', Elvis Presley's 'Hound Dog', 'Just A Closer Walk With Thee', 'Somewhere Over the Rainbow' and 'The Stars and Stripes Forever'.

THE GREATEST SHOW ON EARTH

From their exuberant playing, we hurtled east again to celebrate love in Bollywood style. Some of the Bollywood dancers had flown in from India and were joined by local dancers from the Edinburgh Mela and the Tattoo in a vibrant display of colour and movement in a classic Bollywood 'boy meets girl' story.

We came firmly back to Scotland for the pipes and drums, the dancers, the fiddlers and the band of the Royal Regiment of Scotland to play Scott Skinner's beautiful tribute to Major General Sir Hector Macdonald, 'Hector the Hero'. Major Steven Small, the Director of Army Bagpipe Music, stepped on to the Esplanade to show that he had not become desk-bound, playing first the small pipes then the Highland pipes in this most moving of Scottish melodies.

The hugely entertaining precision of the Top Secret Drummers from Switzerland returned this time with flaming drumsticks and a large number of Swiss visitors each night, before the massed bands of the Royal Air Force saluted the pilots who fought the Battle of Britain in 1940 on their 75th anniversary. The Queen's Colour Squadron of the RAF performed a drill display designed to illustrate the Spitfire squadrons preparing for and fighting the battle in the air.

Unusually, we had three Guards of Honour marching in quick succession: the United States Air Force Honor Guard, the Queen's Colour Squadron and the Royal Scots Dragoon Guards, as well as the always popular Shetland pony mascot of the Royal Regiment of

One of the dancers from India.

Scotland, Lance Corporal Cruachan the Fourth and his Pony Major Corporal Mark Wilkinson. Lance Corporal Cruachan did not appear every night and when I asked Corporal Wilkinson where they had been he replied that he had been commanded to be at Balmoral Castle at the request of Her Majesty the Queen. There is no arguing with a command like that.

Squadron Leader Matthew Little rounded off the main part of the show with a new and appropriate song, 'Arrive as Strangers, Leave as Friends', before the audience proved it by singing and then giving the biggest cheer of the night to 'Auld Lang Syne'.

2016
We started 2016 by taking the Tattoo back to Australia and New Zealand and there is more about that in Act Nine.

It seems scarcely believable that I have reached my 25th year telling the story of each Tattoo up on the Esplanade. It has been a thrilling experience so far and as I sit in the narrator's chair above the Royal Box I am looking forward to seeing old friends again: friends in the New

Zealand Army Band and the Lochiel Marching Team, the Shetland Fiddlers and the Tattoo Dancers, the Imps, the Band and the Drill Team of the King of Norway's Guard, the Jordanian Armed Forces Band and the Massed Pipes and Drums (which always has a different mix each year) and the Military Bands of the Household Cavalry, the Royal Artillery, the Royal Regiment of Scotland, Rifles and the Royal Marines. I am looking forward to the new performers and new performances. For the first time, the Nepal Army Band will perform, bringing back memories of the Coronation year ascent of Mount Everest by Sir Edmund Hilary and Sherpa Tensing Norgay and the United States Army Band Europe which was created for Her Majesty the Queen's first visit to America in 1957. The Scottish State Coach returns to the Tattoo for the first time since 2002, the coach and its mounted escorts processing as they did in 1953 when Her Majesty came to Scotland as the new Queen after her coronation.

Edinburgh Military Tattoo Overseas

NEW ZEALAND 2000
Salute to New Zealand

Although staff from the Tattoo had gone abroad in the past to pass on their expertise, the show itself had not travelled as a compete entertainment until Brigadier Mel Jameson decided, with the blessing of the Board, to accept an invitation from the New Zealand Festival of the Arts to play a part in the Millennium Festival in Wellington in March 2000.

I rather looked forward to the visit, having already been to New Zealand several times. The first was in 1961 when the P&O liner *Iberia*, on which I was returning to Scotland after spending seven years in Australia, had to stop in Auckland for a week for a boiler repair.

I returned in the 1980s as a member of the European Parliament's delegation for relations with the Parliaments of New Zealand and Australia.

The programme for the Tattoo's first visit to New Zealand.

On two or three visits, as well as our meetings with New Zealand parliamentarians, we were able to see quite a lot of the North and South Islands and get to know a fair bit about the country. We also learnt about the culture which had evolved from the settling of European emigrants, many of them from Scotland, among the Maori, who themselves had come to New Zealand in the 13th and 14th centuries. Happily, this helped a great deal when I came to write the script for this giant step beyond the boundaries of the small area of Edinburgh Castle.

Wellington is a compact city, named after the victor of Waterloo, the Duke of Wellington, and built on the slopes of hills around a substantial harbour bay but even this cannot protect the city from its unpredictable weather which was to play its part in the 2000 Tattoo.

Not only was this the first time that The Edinburgh Military Tattoo had travelled outside Scotland, it was also the first time that such a large contingent of British military musicians had travelled abroad since the Second World War and it was the first time that the Edinburgh Military Tattoo had been to New Zealand, where so many Scots had made new homes.

We had an early indication of the hazards which always stalk long-distance multiple journeys. The British Caledonian plane which we were to take from Edinburgh on 2 March was cancelled at short notice because the co-pilot had a detached retina. It meant a two-hour wait for the next one and then, of course, two hours less for the change-over to the next flight, which was heading west across the Atlantic and on through Los Angeles to Auckland.

Everyone on the plane from Edinburgh was on edge and we arrived in London with half an hour to get from Terminal One to Terminal Three. After ten years in the European Parliament swapping planes every week, I was still familiar with Heathrow as it was then and, racing through the corridors, I reached the Air New Zealand plane. I explained the dilemma and to their enormous credit the crew were flexible and all but one of the passengers from Edinburgh made it. The Musical Advisor had left his credit cards on the plane from Edinburgh and stayed behind to try to retrieve them. I do not think he got them back.

It was a very long journey to Los Angeles and on to Auckland where we landed at

5.30am. The plane had been loaded alphabetically and I had been sandwiched in a middle seat surrounded by pipers and drummers intent on anaesthetising themselves with alcohol for the journey. When I was finally able to unwind myself at the end of the flight across the Pacific, I only went to the baggage hall out of curiosity, not expecting my case to have had any chance of arriving. I stared at the familiar case for a while when it appeared on the belt before I accepted that it really was there, goodness knows how, and we progressed on to Wellington.

We were to be visited by the Lord Provost of the City of Edinburgh, Councillor Eric Milligan. After the visit a Black Watch officer, Major Jamie Erskine, who was Officer Commanding the troops, had to carry back the City's heavy and very valuable chain of office in a special belt, as well as bringing home the Lord Provost's suitcase full of the civic gifts presented to him on his visit. This raised some eyebrows among the customs officers.

The show was to be held in the Westpac Trust Stadium,

Building Edinburgh Castle in Wellington, New Zealand.

which had been built the year before on surplus railway land along the waterfront, but set back across the road from the wharf area. The stadium was constructed to accommodate most big sporting events including both codes of rugby, football and cricket and had only opened two months before we arrived.

The organisers had cut off about a quarter of the stadium at one end to build a replica of Edinburgh Castle for the Tattoo and it was a wonderfully realistic backdrop against which to stage the event. It had the advantage for the Tattoo of having three exits – two at either side as well as the gatehouse in the centre

– unlike the real Edinburgh Castle, which has only two. As I glanced at it out of the corner of my eye whilst introducing the items, I was aware of how realistic it was and began to wonder what the patch of green, the grass of the stadium, was doing in front of it.

Getting an audience had not been a problem. We had already been asked if we would stage an extra performance to help satisfy the demand for tickets and even those extra tickets went within a few hours.

We had the luxury of four days of rehearsals before the first show on Friday 10 March. As I introduced it, I decided on the spur of the moment to try to get the audience to sing 'Happy Birthday' as I did in Edinburgh. Glancing around the room in which I was speaking, I caught sight of the Musical Advisor, Lieutenant Colonel David Price, and instantly decided that we would celebrate his birthday. After all, I thought, who in that huge audience would know? That went well, the audience sang and we started the show. It was not until a couple of days later that we saw in *The*

Dominion, the Wellington newspaper, that there had been a boy called David Price from Lower Hutt in the audience to celebrate his 12th birthday and the assiduous paper had brought the two together in the Park Royal Hotel for a photograph. Shooting from the lip can have its hazards.

The first show opened with a Maori greeting, the *Karanga* (a female vocal call), followed by a *Whaikorero* (a male oratorical piece) and a conch shell fanfare. These were followed by 'The Herding Song' played from the gatehouse of the mock Castle by Corporal Alastair Duthie of the Black Watch, who hailed from South Canterbury. The trumpeters on the gatehouse played Scotland's Salute to New Zealand 'Jubilee' before the pipers and drummers came pouring out of the three entrances on to the field.

We had brought with us the pipes and drums of the Royal Scots Dragoon Guards, the Scots Guards, the Royal Scots, the Black Watch, the Kings Own Scottish Borders and the Argyll and Sutherland Highlanders. We added in New Zealand the Champions of Otago,

the City of Auckland,
the City of Dunedin,
the City of Invercargill,
the City of Wellington,
Dalewool Auckland and
District, the New Zealand
Police and Temuka.

As the pipers marched
away in their kilts, from half
a world away from Scotland
came the Band of the Fiji
Defence Force in their *sulus*,
the Fijian national dress and
the Melanesian equivalent
of the kilt. The band had
played on the Esplanade of
Edinburgh Castle two years
earlier and here they were
on their own side of the
world playing the music of
Melanesia at the Edinburgh
Tattoo in Wellington. Once
again, they brought their
traditional victory dance after
an epic battle in ancient Fiji
– the Meke – a spear dance
performed by huge warriors
in grass skirts. The Fijians'
Bandmaster, Lieutenant
Nangoo Drew Nee Dhoi,
conducted the band in a song
unrivalled in the affections
of all Fijians, 'Isa Lei', before
Drum Major Dhau Thacka
Thacka led the band away to
'Tukuna Noqu I Loloma'.

The Lochiel Marching
Team is based in Wellington,
so they were completely at
home and enchanted the
big Westpac Stadium home
crowds with an immaculate
seven minute display on their
fifth Tattoo appearance.
Right behind them came the
New Zealand Army Band
who raced through another
breathtakingly energetic
performance under their
Director of Music, Captain
Dave Clearwater. It was good
experience for the bandmaster,
Staff Sergeant Graham
Hickman, who was to lead
the band at the same stadium
when the Tattoo returned
to Wellington in 2016.

Some 200 of the finest
Highland dancers drawn from
all over New Zealand danced
reels and the Highland fling
in the shape of a St Andrews
cross, with sword dances filling
the four quarters of the saltire.

Then the combined Bands
of the Royal New Zealand
Navy, the New Zealand
Army and the Royal New
Zealand Air Force marched
on to the appropriately chosen
Wellington and entertained
the crowds with music
highlighting their services.

The Aotearoa Traditional
Maori Performing Arts Society
from Rotorua brought the

vibrancy of Maori culture to the Tattoo with their portrayal of the Great Canoe Migration of the Maori, which they celebrated in a Poi Dance, an Action Song, and the fearsome war dance – the Haka.

Four of the finest British military bands, the Scots Guards, the Royal Marines and the Lowland and the Highland Bands of the Scottish Division played a marvellously varied programme of favourite tunes. Combining then with the New Zealand bands in the theme of the Rugby Union World Cup, the World in Union, we enjoyed the glorious singing of Joanna Heslop and the Samoan Lota Nu'u Choir, based in Wellington, who followed with the unofficial national song of New Zealand 'Pokare Kare Ana'.

After the two national anthems had been played, the performance was rounded off, as it is in Edinburgh, by the playing of the Lone Piper. This was done by WO1 Bruce Hitchings MBE, BEM, the Senior Pipe Major of the British Army who had been born in Palmerston North and who was playing his last show before he retired from the Army.

This all worked effectively until the last night when Wellington's weather came roaring in with a vengeance. Each night the performance started at 8.30pm. On the final night on Monday 13 March, the rain started at 8.10pm and did not let up all night. The rain was heavy and it was accompanied by a high wind. The lights for the show had been strung on cables running the length of the arena and I noticed that these were swaying precariously in the gusting wind. I was afraid that if they snapped they would crash down on the performers and I spent the entire show with my hand on the microphone key ready, if the worst should happen, to shout to the performers 'Look up and move!'S Thankfully, the riggers had done a good job and the cables stayed intact.

As the evening wore on, the Producer eventually said, 'We are going to have to cut this.' I waited for his choice of what to cut, but he said nothing more. So, grabbing the bull by the horns, I decided that we should cut straight from the national anthems to the march off. It meant missing a speech by the Lord Provost, the singing of 'Auld Lang Syne', the bands playing 'Now is the Hour' and 'Sunset', the Lone Piper playing 'My Home' and Sir Walter Scott's lines from 'The Lay of the Last Minstrel'. The flagpole carrying the two national flags on top of the tower where the Lone Piper played had already disappeared in the high wind, so that would have been dangerous in any event. There were no communications from the production box to the Principal Director of Music, Lieutenant Colonel Richard Waterer OBE, out on the field, so I had to devise an announcement which would be clear to him and the performers and not obvious to the audience and I had to do it quickly. Happily, it worked and the sodden performers were able to seek shelter about ten minutes earlier than usual. We were leaving the next day and the musicians all had to pack their wet kit as soon as they returned to their accommodation. I do not believe any of it survived the journey back in a fit state.

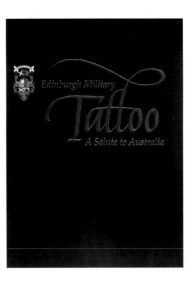

The programme for the Tattoo's first visit to Australia.

Australia 2005
A Salute To Australia

Five years later and we were off down under again, this time to Sydney's Aussie Stadium in Australia. On this visit, however, we were to do more than the Tattoo.

I had spent Christmas in the United States of America visiting my elder son Tom and his American wife. Visiting my daughter-in-law's parents, a front tooth broke while I was eating a harder than expected dessert. I was not worried about the appearance, but was anxious about how my voice would sound. I flew in to Manchester on the 6th of January and took a bus straight to an excellent dentist at Northenden. He made a temporary repair and I flew on to Scotland at lunch-time. I drove back 12 days later for a slightly more permanent fix. With a bit of care it worked.

We left on 22 January heading first for Canberra to be there in time to celebrate Australia Day on 26 January with an 'Australia Day Tribute' in front of the Australian War Memorial. The celebrations had been going on at the War Memorial from 3.00pm with local bands playing a series of little concerts all compered by a well-known Australian television newsreader Ross Symonds. As we approached 7.00pm Ross introduced the Prime Minister John Howard and the Governor General Major General Michael Jeffrey. I was also introduced to the Royal Australian Air Force Roulettes – the equivalent of the RAF Red Arrows – which flew straight up the line of ANZAC Parade and over the top of the War Memorial.

Sitting beside Ross in a little tent with a pretty good view of all that was going on, I introduced the Tattoo contingent marching up ANZAC Parade towards the War Memorial, the pipes and drums and military bands from the United Kingdom and the Queens Colour Squadron of the Royal Air Force. In the relative cool of a fine Australian summer evening, they played what was in effect a mini-tattoo before the Governor General gave Squadron Leader Paul Rooney of the Queen's Colour Squadron permission to march away.

The next day we all moved to Sydney for the full Tattoo at the Aussie Stadium. Sydney was hot, especially for folk from Scotland who had flown from their winter straight into the Australian summer. We did not mind, but had to be canny about not giving careless impressions of a team of boiled lobsters.

On the opening day the *Sydney Morning Herald* declared that people should 'forget tenors like Pavarotti or pop divas like Madonna. When it comes to the world of entertainment, there's no star bigger or more enduring than Edinburgh Castle'. Like Wellington the organisers in Sydney had built another replica of the Castle at one end of the Aussie Stadium. It too looked spectacular and after standing up well to a torrential downpour on the first evening of rehearsals, it provided the ideal backdrop for our first visit to Australia when the huge show opened on 3 February.

The publicists for the tattoo had seen what we did in Edinburgh when welcoming people before the show and singing Happy Birthday and had managed to encourage people to ask for welcomes. So I did not have to try to find a birthday from a standing start as I had done in Wellington and the big audiences joined in with gusto. The messages were a good indication of how many people loved the Tattoo on television but for one reason or another could not get to Scotland to see it in Edinburgh, so this was a golden opportunity that they did not want to miss.

Each member of the audience had been issued with a glow stick, except on the last night when they ran out. I thought that if these were just lit at random the effect would be lost so I asked the audience to have a little rehearsal with the sticks but wait for my suggestion for the best time to light them. Happily, the audience took the suggestion to heart and we had a spectacular display at what I thought was the best place for them in the show.

We were honoured by a distinguished series of Guests of Honour: the Lord Provost of Edinburgh Councillor, Lesley Hinds; the British High Commissioner in Australia, Sir Alastair Goodlad; the Governor of New South Wales Professor, Marie Bashir, whose husband Sir Nicholas Shehadie had been

The finale of the 2005 Tattoo in Sydney's Aussie Stadium.

Lord Mayor of Sydney and had won 30 caps playing for the Australian Rugby Union team; the Governor General Major General Michael Jeffery and the Chief of the Australian Defence Force General Peter Cosgrove, who was to become Governor General nine years later.

The Tattoo opened with an aboriginal 'smoking' ceremony in which the ground was cleansed of bad spirits with the smoke of gum leaves as Matthew Doyle played the didgeridoo. Then the trumpeters on the Castle played 'the Salute to Australia', a skilfully arranged blend of 'Scotland the Brave' and 'Waltzing Matilda', before the Massed Pipes and Drums emerged from the three entrances to fill the wide grass arena, which was normally home to both codes of rugby and football matches. The Stadium was a near neighbour of Sydney Cricket Ground.

We had brought seven pipe bands from the United Kingdom services, plus a police pipe band to join seven Australian pipe bands; they made a big sound around the huge stadium. After a well received programme

of Scottish tunes they all marched off to Jack O'Hagan's thoroughly Australian 'Road to Gundagai'.

The effervescent New Zealand Army Band thrilled the big crowds with their variety of music, even including 'Dorothy the Dinosaur' from the Australian children's band, The Wiggles. The free-roaming New Zealanders were followed by the sharp precision of the Queen's Colour Squadron of the Royal Air Force's precision drill display. The finest dancers drawn from all over Australia joined the Edinburgh Tattoo Highland Ceilidh Dancers in one of the largest displays of Highland dancing ever seen in the country as they danced a tribute to Scotland. I rather enjoyed this presentation, which had been danced at Edinburgh in 1997. It needed carefully timed narration describing Scotland, a well co-ordinated triumph of music, movement and the voice.

The immaculate young conscripts of the King of Norway's Guard produced yet another faultless display of marching, silent drill and music and then we moved to an act which we could never show in Edinburgh, because there is not enough space on the Esplanade. This was a display by the riders of the New South Wales Police. The Mounted Unit was formed in 1825 by the Governor of the state, Sir Thomas Brisbane, to deal with the problems caused by escaping convicts who fled into the bush to form gangs of bushrangers.

The unit gave its first musical 'drill and sword display' at the Sydney Show in 1895 and in 2005 gave an intricate demonstration of their skills in 12 manoeuvres on the big grass arena with passes, cross-overs, wheels and a dramatic charge at the end. The NSW Police riders were followed by another percussion display by the Top Secret Drummers from Switzerland.

It was not a battle of the bands, but the bands representing the three armed services of Australia: the Sydney detachment of the Royal Australian Navy Band, the Australian Army Band Sydney and the Air Command Band Sydney. These three bands played a full programme of well known Australian tunes including 'Happy Little Vegemites'. They were immediately followed by three United Kingdom bands representing all three services: Scots Guards, Her Majesty's Royal Marines Scotland and the Central Band of the Royal Air Force. They then combined in 'The World in Union' and 'I Still Call Australia Home'. To round it off, Australian Army Musician Deborah Cotton sang 'Waltzing Matilda' as the dancers brought on a huge Australian flag.

As if that weren't dramatic enough, after the Bands had played 'Land of Hope and Glory' enriched by the beautiful voice of Allegra Giagu and the Tattoo Choir, more dancers carried on a giant Union Flag. The bands and pipes and drums played 'The Bonnie Lass of Fyvie' and Scott Skinner's intensely moving 'Hector the Hero', and then it was time for the glow sticks.

I told the audience, 'Now is the time to switch your glow sticks on, let them shine out and sway in time to the music as Lt Col Patrick Pickett conducts 'I am Australian'. And shine out they did. Some 28,000 glow sticks lit up and swayed gently in time to the immensely popular Australian song, written in 1987 by

The programme
for the Tattoo's
second visit
to Australia,
celebrating
60 years of
Valour, Mateship
and Glory.

Bruce Woodley of the Seekers and Dobe Newton of the Bushwackers. There have even been calls for it to become Australia's national anthem and at this Tattoo it galvanised the audiences as Sergeant Russell Paynter introduced the song with a didgeridoo and singers from all three Australian services filled the stadium with the historical and cultural lyrics which have made the song so popular.

After Auld Lang Syne, both National Anthems, the Lone Piper and Sir Walter Scott's nostalgic words, a huge display of fireworks shot into the night sky from the wave shaped roof of the stadium to bring this first visit to Australia to a memorable close.

Australia 2010 Celebrating 60 Years Of Valour, Mateship, Glory

Five years later in February 2010, the Tattoo returned to the same stadium in Sydney which had acquired a different name(the Sydney Football Stadium), but more importantly for us, the Tattoo had acquired a new name with the Royal prefix becoming The Royal Edinburgh Military Tattoo. So, as it happened, the

Edinburgh Military

Tattoo

Celebrating 60 years of Valour, Mateship, Glory

Tattoo's first performances as Royal took place in Australia as we recalled the strong links between Britain and Australia during the 60 years of the Tattoo's history.

It was another memorable show and this time, on the second night, I even had to make a proposal of marriage. This is an annual occurrence in Edinburgh, but I had not expected it in Sydney. A gentleman from Perth, Western Australia had flown in with his girlfriend who had emigrated from Scotland when she was just a lassie, and she and her family with her prospective fiancée, had all come to see the show. I do not know if she was expecting it, but the proposal went booming round the Stadium and I hope they are happily married.

We were honoured with more distinguished Salute Takers, the Governor of New South Wales, Professor

Marie Bashir who had been with us five years earlier, the Lord Provost of the City of Edinburgh, Councillor George Grubb, the Governor General, Mrs Quentin Bryce and the Chief of the Australian Defence Force, Air Chief Marshal Angus Houston.

We received an aboriginal welcome with a didgeridoo and clapper sticks, which led into the fanfare 'The Gathering'. After the Massed Pipes and Drums, Russia's musical ambassadors, the Band of the Moscow Military Conservatoire, brought a distinctly high-quality Russian sound to the stadium. Australia's best Highland dancers followed with a demonstration of just how far Highland dancing has developed and where it might be going in a programme intriguingly called *Steaming Reels and Other Stories.*

The New Zealand Army Band gave us another iconoclastic performance and we followed with the group which I had first met in a little tattoo in Springfield, Massachusetts, 15 years earlier – the Middlesex County Volunteers Fifes & Drums from the Boston area

of the United States, who had made their Edinburgh debut in 2007. In Sydney, they were wearing the uniforms of the American War for Independence of the late 18th century, drilling and playing music from that period.

Like The Royal Edinburgh Military Tattoo, the Military Band of the People's Liberation Army of China was 60 years old in 2010, so we were delighted to share a birthday with them and welcome them to Sydney where they began with the appropriate tune as a toast 'Drink One More Cup of Wine' and formed the figure 60.

The New South Wales Mounted Police returned and demonstrated just how skilled are the riders and how well trained are the horses. The displays were not only similar to the ones we had seen five years earlier, but the calm way in which they walked beside the marching bands also made an impressive spectacle; the State of New South Wales has always bred fine horses. For many years the horses of British cavalry troopers came from New South Wales which gave their mounts the name of Walers. The horses on the

Tattoo – the same horses which patrol the streets of Sydney – had been purchased or donated and included a variety of breeds, ranging from Thoroughbreds, such as the race horse Patezza (the Winner of the 2005 Doncaster Cup), to Clydesdale-cross horses (once used for heavy work such as ploughing fields).

The irrepressible Trinidad and Tobago Defence Force Steel Orchestra and Drums, under their Director of Music WO2 Robert Tobitt and Drum Major Sergeant William Mapp, brought the sunshine and the sound of the Caribbean to the stadium. The Band and Drill Team of His Majesty the King's Guard from Norway and the Top Secret Drum Corps from Switzerland then took the Tattoo back to Europe.

The Bands representing the armed services of Australia and the United Kingdom marched out to that most appropriate of marches by the long serving Director of Music of the Coldstream Guards and the Brigade of Guards, John Mackenzie Rogan, 'Bond of Friendship'.

The groups each played their most appropriate music before the band members moved forward to light candles in order to mark the first anniversary of the devastating Black Saturday bushfires which had ravaged the State of Victoria and killed 173 people a year earlier. Their action was to remember the courage and sacrifice of the civilian community as well as those in the military forces who stood ready to show outstanding valour in times of great peril. The candles, which carried the flame which could destroy, were also a sign of remembrance and hope.

Amongst the more familiar finale music of 'I Still Call Australia Home', Colonel Bogey, Highland Cathedral and Waltzing Matilda, was a new tune composed by Pipe Major Roddy McDonald of the Queensland Police, 'With Honour We Serve'. As the bands played, 12 pairs of soldiers in modern uniforms slow marched on to the arena with flaming torches. They were joined by six horses and their riders in the uniforms of the Australian Light Horse, whose charge had scattered the Turks at Beersheba in 1917. Four of the horses stood and two lay down as their predecessors would have done when their riders were forced to stop and defend themselves from an attacking enemy.

Sgt James Scott of the Coldstream Guards sang 'Here's to the Heroes' as the Evening Hymn, which seemed an appropriate note on which to close our celebration of 60 years of Valour, Mateship and Glory.

Australia and New Zealand 2016; Fanfare for the Future, Melbourne and Wellington

Brigadier David Allfrey, the Tattoo's Producer since 2011, has always believed in the ambassadorial role which the Tattoo can play on the world stage and five years after he took the reins of the Tattoo, he steered the great show back down under, this time to two venues in both Australia and New Zealand.

While Britain turned up the central heating, we went into a southern hemisphere summer again. We headed first to Melbourne and the Etihad Stadium, built close to the water in an old docklands area, to present five shows indoors with the roof closed. Although we are accustomed to working out of doors whatever the weather, that at least allowed us to control the lighting effects and manage the sound. In Wellington, we returned to the Westpac Trust Stadium and played out of doors, but this time the lighting was placed around the stadium and the weather was much kinder.

I had lived in Melbourne as a teenager when I worked as an office boy for an advertising agency (which allowed me to get to know the layout of the city very well) and then later as a reporter for *The Age* newspaper. As a Member of the European Parliament, I had visited the ANZAC Memorial on ANZAC Day in 1988, where I was enormously honoured to meet the only man to win two Victoria Crosses in the Second World War – New Zealander Captain Charlie Upham. I had also gone to Melbourne in 2001 to present a *Scotland the Brave* concert, so I was returning to fairly familiar territory where many of the landmarks were the same, but also to a city which had changed considerably. I had never seen the stadium, so there was plenty of exploring to be done to get to know the quickest ways of moving from our accommodation to the show. As I said earlier, I had also visited Wellington in 1961 on my way back to Scotland and again in the 1980s as a member of the European Parliament's delegation before I had gone back to present the Tattoo there in 2000.

Once again, we had superb replicas of Edinburgh Castle built at one end of each arena and more distinguished Salute Takers including, in Melbourne, the Governor General, the Governor of the State of Victoria, the Lord Mayor of Melbourne and service chiefs and in Wellington the Governor General, the Deputy Prime Minister, the Chief of the Defence Force and the Mayor of Wellington.

The theme of the Tattoo titled *Fanfare for the Future* was a reflection of the importance of the Australian and New Zealand contribution to the Gallipoli campaign as the ANZACs. It started with the last shot being fired as the ANZAC troops slipped away from Turkish soil in the dark of a December night. The entire evacuation was one of the most remarkable

operations in military history. In 1990, I had had the good fortune to speak to an elderly man who had fought at Gallipoli with the King's Own Scottish Borderers in 1915 and had been evacuated on New Year's Day 1916. I had also spoken at length to a Turkish academic, whose grandfather had been an officer in the Turkish Navy and who understood the tenacity with which the Turkish soldiers fought for their land and the skill of their leader Mustafa Kemal. As a result, I had a clear vision from both descriptions of what Gallipoli had felt like for men on the ground. It was a challenge to write a clear and tightly concise version of the campaign leading up to that final shot delivered by a clever if fairly crude mechanical device of dripping water. Rifles kept firing after the Allied troops had left and persuaded the Turks that the British and ANZAC troops were still active.

As that shot rang out across the arenas in Melbourne and Wellington, the Tattoo looked back a century to the time when the two countries came of age and after a pause, the lights brought up the dawn of a new day. The trumpeters played the Fanfare for the Future before the massed pipes and drums marched out of the three Castle entrances with tunes from both hemispheres. As they marched away in Melbourne, they left behind the Pipes and Drums of the Australian Defence Force wearing their newly created ADF tartan. These pipers and drummers had been specially formed from all three services by the ADF and the Tattoo, and marched away to the cheers of the crowd playing the Road to Gundagai. In Wellington they all marched off to 'God Defend New Zealand'.

The Lochiel Marching Team from Wellington, by now 35-time National Marching Champions, gave us another impeccable display to the music from Lord of the Rings, filmed in New Zealand, before we moved north to the Pacific islands of Tonga and Fiji.

The Tongans must have the only working Director of Music who is a member of the House of Lords in the now elevated Lieutenant Colonel Lord Ve'ehala. The Royal Corps of Musicians played some of the islands' music and happily included the graceful Tau'olunga hand dancing before the fiercer Fijian Military Forces Band played their music from Melanesia in Butukatun Raranivaru. Both bands combined and added Maori performers from New Zealand and drummers from the pipe bands to roll the sound of the waves on the shore as they played and sang the praises of the Pacific fish found to the north of New Zealand, the Tarakihi.

Fiddlers from opposite sides of the world came together as the Hjaltibonhoga Fiddlers from Shetland, Melbourne Scottish Fiddlers in Melbourne and New Zealand's Hjaltibonhoga Fiddlers in Wellington played a lively set of traditional Shetland tunes in excellent harmony. The Tattoo Highland Dancers met their Australian and New Zealand counterparts in their respective countries for a lively display of contemporary Highland dancing, beautifully choreographed by the former World Champion dancer Aileen Robertson.

In 1836, South Australia began to be settled as a colony of free settlers. No police were sent to what was hoped would be a law-abiding society, however, with fears about the arrival of escaped convicts from other states, the South Australia Police service was established two years later as the first in Australia, and the third in the world. The South Australia Police had established a fine band which had been to the Tattoo in Edinburgh in 1990, 2000 and 2010 and now only had to travel to the neighbouring state of Victoria and cross the Tasman to Wellington to play another largely Australian programme.

From the time when Gods communed with man, Maori histories recall the Polynesian ancestor Maui. Among his many great achievements, he fished up the North Island of New Zealand. Maui was renowned for his quickness of mind, his ability to transform circumstance and his prodigious creativity. It was to the North Island, the fish of Maui, that the Maori came. The mighty New Zealand All Blacks have brought the Maori Haka to the world. In Melbourne, the leading Kapa Haka group Te Whanau a Apanui from the North Island of New Zealand created a truly authentic Kapa Haka and in Wellington eight groups came together to create a remarkable spectacle of movement and singing from a large group in traditional Maori dress.

The Maori who came from Hawaiki in the 13th century were known as the Vikings of the Sunrise. More than 500 years earlier than the Maori migration to New Zealand, the Vikings from Norway had swept down on Scotland as invaders. But all is peaceful now and we could welcome the Band and Drill Team of His Majesty the King's Guard from Norway, the land of Fiords and the Midnight Sun, whose young conscripts gave their huge audiences another immaculate performance of music and drill.

Since we were down under, we could not have done a show without the always popular New Zealand Army Band. The Drum Major Staff Sergeant Tristan Mitchell always carried a Maori Tewhatewha – which he had carved himself – as his mace and in Wellington he presented a Tewhatewha of his own creation each night to the Salute Taker. On the first night, he presented his Tewhatewha to the Governor

General, Lieutenant General the Right Honourable Sir Jerry Mateparae, a former Chief of the New Zealand Defence Force and of Maori origin. Sir Jerry handed it back, asking Staff Sergeant Mitchell to carry it to Her Majesty's 90th birthday celebrations in Windsor and to the Tattoo in the Edinburgh before he returned it when the band came home again.

I also had great pleasure in being able to wish Tristan's father Maurice, from Westport on the west coast of the South Island, a very Happy 72nd Birthday in front of the huge audience when his parents came to the show. I did not see it, but I believe Mr Mitchell senior stood up and waved to the crowd when he heard his 'shout out'.

The show returned to a reflective mood as the Massed Pipes and Drums with the aid of the fiddlers, some of the dancers, the small pipes of the Director of Army Bagpipe Music, Major Steven Small, and the singing of Squadron Leader Matt Little played Scott Skinner's beautiful tribute to Major General Sir Hector Macdonald, Hector the Hero.

Then the literally flaming drumsticks of the Top Secret drummers brought the two stadiums alive. Dropping drumsticks is an occupational hazard for these lightning-fast percussionists but they are never without a drumstick and from a quiver of spare sticks, carried unobtrusively beside their drums, they can immediately replace any that go down.

Then, in Australia, the Australian Tri-Service Military Bands and, in New Zealand, the Bands of the New Zealand Defence Force, played their distinctive programmes followed by the British Military Bands from all three services with a medley of British music. Then they were joined by all the other Bands from Norway, Fiji, Tonga and South Australia. Accompanied by local choirs, the pipes and drums added to the huge sound with Mark Knopfler's 'Going Home' from the film *Local Hero*.

In Melbourne, the stage crew had to make a new podium quickly to allow the Principal Director of Music, Lieutenant Colonel Nick Grace, to mount the steps comfortably in order to conduct 'Going Home' as it was obvious that the first set of steps had been designed for someone taller.

Once the rest of the cast was assembled, and in particular the dancers, the bands led into a party with the chart-topping Men at Work single 'Land Down Under', the Martha and Vandellas' hit 'Dancing in the Street', the Bee Gees' 'You Should be Dancing', Michael Jackson's 'Thriller', Robbie Williams' 'Let Me Entertain You' and Pharrell Williams' 'Happy'.

Squadron Leader Matt Little, the Director of Music of the RAF College Band, thought I should replicate the Vincent Price narration during the short section of 'Thriller', so I jotted down the macabre words, shortened them to four lines, listened carefully to the way Vincent Price had recorded his narration for the 'Thriller' video and added the words over the intro as the dancers replicated the movement of the ghoulish figures. It must have worked, for one of the ladies acting as a liaison officer for some of the performers in New Zealand asked if I was adding the narration to

'Thriller' or if it had been a recording of Vincent Price. I took that as high praise.

The shows closed with the playing of the National Anthems, the singing of 'Isa Lei' and 'Auld Lang Syne', 'the Evening Hymn', the Lone Piper and the words of Sir Walter Scott. The audience applause and reaction, with a standing ovation at the end of the first show in Melbourne, suggested that the huge crowds had appreciated what we had done and very clearly vindicated the Producer's belief in The Royal Edinburgh Military Tattoo as a force for good far beyond the borders of Scotland.

After we had returned home and begun to think about the August event, we were thrilled and flattered when the DVD of the Tattoo was released a couple of months later. It shot straight to Number One in the Australian Aria DVD music charts, leaving Andre Rieu, Andrea Bocelli, Sir Cliff Richard and Adele trailing it its wake.

Mini Tattoos and Others in the UK

EVEN BEFORE THE main Tattoo started to sell out in 1999, it had always been ready to send performers out to places from which it was difficult for people to travel to the Tattoo.

We did a mini-Tattoo each year on the lawn outside the former Princess Margaret Rose Orthopaedic Hospital at Fairmilehead in Edinburgh. It had been opened in 1932 as the Edinburgh Hospital for Crippled Children and renamed for the Queen's younger sister, Princess Margaret. After the Second World War, it moved its focus to post-accident orthopaedic surgery and rehabilitation, mainly dealing with the victims of traffic accidents, and became a centre for research and development, including the first electrically-powered prosthetic arms. It closed in 2000 when its work was re-assigned to the new Edinburgh Royal Infirmary and the land was sold for more houses.

There was always a great pleasure in going to the hospital, whose patients were unable to be moved to the Esplanade, and to see how much they appreciated the Tattoo coming to them.

The Tattoo had always sent contingents of pipes and drums to entertain the residents of Erskine Hospital down at Erskine on the south bank of the River Clyde west of Glasgow. Erskine is a remarkable establishment which was established in 1916 to manage the large numbers of wounded and limbless men returning to Britain from the battlefields of the First World War. Sir William Macewen, the Regius Professor of Surgery at the University of Glasgow, was the catalyst for the foundation of the Princess Louise Scottish Hospital for Limbless Sailors and Soldiers. Using the mechanical and engineering skills developed in the shipyards of the Clyde, the hospital became a pioneer in the creation of artificial limbs.

Sir John Reid of the North British Locomotive Company had bought Erskine House for the hospital after Sir Thomas Aikman, the owner, had granted the use of the house and 350 acres of grounds for the duration of the war and for a year afterwards in order to establish the new facility. The public had always generously supported the hospital, but in the late 1990s the managers decided it must move to new bespoke premises to meet the changing needs of veterans and the increasingly stringent regulations needed to provide modern medical care. This involved not only erecting new buildings in Erskine's spacious grounds, but also establishing Erskine facilities in other places, which made it a lot easier for relatives to visit the veterans in the hospital's care. Once those were completed, the Tattoo pipers and drummers visited the Erskine homes in Glasgow and Edinburgh each year to bring a little of the Tattoo's magic to them.

Every year the Tattoo has paid a visit to Glasgow's George Square where most of the performers present a shortened version of their acts to the members of the public who crowd into the Square. The Glasgow people were so enthusiastic and keen to see the performers that they never seemed to notice that I was narrating the show, holding a script in one hand, a microphone in the other and trying to see what was happening as well as communicating with the performers. Indeed, they always seemed rather put out when they had to move aside to let the performers enter and leave the little arena in the Square.

There are a dozen statues around George Square, one or two of which have plinths on which I could just about stand to get a view over the heads of the crowd to see the performance. From there, I could announce the next item, but as soon as I would get up and perch precariously on one of the narrow ledges, other people would climb up and crowd in, rather like passengers getting on a bus trying to sit next to the driver. Even having the help of a local Senior Non-Commissioned officer in the TA did not stop them and give me any more room. The Lord Provost, however, always lays on a buffet lunch afterwards in the City Chambers, which rounds the event off nicely for the people who have taken part.

Between 2002 and 2007 the Tattoo received sponsorship from Dewar's World of Whisky, which had a distillery and a visitor centre at Aberfeldy, in Perthshire. On a Sunday during the Tattoo each year, we would journey up to present a free show for local people and visitors.

In 2004, we added little stage performances in the Ross Bandstand in Edinburgh's Princes Street Gardens. In 1460, King James III ordered that the ground be flooded to strengthen the Castle's northern defences. A dam was built at the east end and spring water flowing from St Margaret's Well at the foot of the Castle flooded the little valley. Edinburgh folk would boat there in the summer and skate in the winter but, sadly, it became a convenient dump for every sort of waste and it was drained in 1759. The Ross Bandstand was built in 1877 and gifted to the city by the Chairman of the Distillers Company Ltd, William Ross. Two free Tattoo concerts annually, sponsored for several years by the Royal Bank of Scotland, allowed people who could not get tickets for the sold-out Tattoo to enjoy some of the acts from the terraced seats facing the bandstand.

2009 proved to be a busier year than usual, with four extra smaller Taste of the Tattoo events within a day's return drive from Edinburgh. These were designed to be the Tattoo's contribution to what was billed as the Year of Homecoming which was intended to attract people of Scottish ancestry to visit the country. 2009 had been chosen because it was the 250th anniversary of the birth of the poet Robert Burns. Scotland's culture and heritage was one of the themes of the year and the Tattoo was perfectly designed to fit that.

Taste of the Tattoo events were held in Glasgow, Linlithgow, Cumnock and Jedburgh. As well as the annual mini-tattoo in George Square in Glasgow, mini-tattoos were added on the flat ground below the ruins of Linlithgow Palace in West Lothian, in the forecourt of the

18th-century Adam mansion of Dumfries House some two miles west of Cumnock in South Ayrshire and at Riverside Park, the home of Jedforest Rugby Football Club, in the Scottish Borders. I had not sought a say in the first three venues, but I was determined that the Borders should enjoy something of the Tattoo while I was Convener of the Council and I reckoned that one of our rugby grounds, with enough parking for buses and permanent stands already in place, would take away a lot of the extra headaches which always accompany the planning of these events.

All of the events went off well, attracting big audiences mainly of people who did not have tickets for the Edinburgh event. Glasgow attracted the usual lunchtime crowd, the weather was sunny in Linlithgow, wet in Ayrshire and more or less alright in the Borders. The audiences certainly got a marvellous Taste of the Tattoo in these free events with massed pipes and drums from the United Kingdom and overseas, including the Royal Corps of Musicians from Tonga, the Swiss Army Central Band, the Calgary Burns Club singers from Canada, performers from the province of Shaanxi in the west of China, traditional and contemporary Highland dancing from Scottish and Australian dancers, the Top Secret Drummers from Switzerland and a Royal Air Force Band topping off the shows with 'Amazing Grace'.

In 2014, we spread out again as part of another Year of Homecoming, going on our annual visit to Glasgow. The following week we took the show to the street outside the Thistles Centre in Stirling and a week later to the City Square in Dundee. Those shows attracted good crowds with most of that year's cast getting a chance to see more of Scotland outside Edinburgh and the local people getting a chance to see them. We enlisted the Provost of Stirling Council, Councillor Mike Robbins and the Lord Provost of Dundee, Councillor Bob Duncan to take the salute at the end of the show.

The always popular Top Secret Drummers from Basel.

Howdens Joinery Military Tattoos

Earlier in 2014, the international joinery company Howdens had asked us to provide a mini-Tattoo to entertain the senior members of their staff and their suppliers from 25 countries around the world at their annual suppliers' conference at Gleneagles Hotel with a Howdens Joinery Military Tattoo. The event took place in the five-star hotel's Equestrian Arena with a programme reminiscent of the main Tattoo. We brought in the pipers and drummers of the Royal Scots Borderers First Battalion of the Royal Regiment of Scotland, four local pipe bands and the band of the Royal Regiment of Scotland. 100 Highland dancers, dancing reels and strathspeys, were choreographed by World, Commonwealth, British, Scottish, North American, Canadian and Australian Champion, Rachel McLagan. The bands played 'Highland Cathedral' and 'Western Front' as our tribute to the First World War centenary, after which the guests returned to the hotel for a nightcap.

Howdens must have been happy with the event, for two years later they returned to Gleneagles for another Suppliers' Conference and asked us to provide another mini-Tattoo for their guests. We presented the 2016 show on the much smaller grass circle at the front of the hotel with the pipers and drummers of the Royal Highland Fusiliers Second Battalion, the Royal Regiment of Scotland and the Royal Burgh of Stirling Pipe Band, Highland dancers with Broadswords, and two serving soldiers dancing the Highland Fling. Then the Top Secret drummers from Switzerland flew in to join the cast and the Band of Her Majesty's Royal Marines Scotland. Being outside allowed us to project images on to the front of the hotel and to use fireworks to great effect; afterwards the guests had only a short walk back into the hotel for another night-cap.

The idea of tattoos has remained popular for a very long time. People think they are pretty easy to produce and only find out the amount of work which is involved when they try to put them on. I have seen many appear with high hopes and good will and disappear almost as quickly. But some have outlasted the first appearance and become popular and I have been lucky enough to present a number of these in addition to Edinburgh.

Berwick Military Tattoos 1994–2005

When a group of folk in Berwick-upon-Tweed were searching for a way to extend the tourist season, they hit upon the idea of using the old Barracks as an ideal location for a small Tattoo. And so in 1994 the first Berwick Tattoo was held to wide congratulations and declarations that it was far better than Edinburgh. The show was to last for 12 years before the costs began to outrun the income and with great reluctance the Tattoo Trust decided it had to end. I had the good fortune to be able to present all of the shows which were held on Saturday and Sunday evenings to allow TA performers to take part.

Berwick Barracks was the home of the King's Own Scottish Borderers, so it was entirely appropriate that the first people on to the Barrack Square in the first show in 1994 were the pipers and drummers of the KOSB, joined by their colleagues from the Scottish Transport Regiment. The most notable piper in the long history of the KOSB was Daniel Laidlaw, who won a Victoria Cross for his outstanding courage piping the men out of the trenches at the Battle of Loos in 1915. It was moving that on this first Berwick Tattoo the pipes he played at Loos were played by Private Kevin Turnbull from Selkirk.

The county of Northumberland has had a long association with the Fusiliers, dating back to 1674 and the raising of the fifth Foot. So it was fitting that we should welcome the Northumberland Band of the Royal Regiment of Fusiliers and the Corps of Drums of the 6th (Northumberland) Battalion of the RRF. Most people think of square bashing in a barracks but of course, military drill had an important purpose in battle. To remind us of just how the soldiers of yesterday manoeuvred the 68th Foot Display Team, dressed in the carefully researched uniforms of the early 19th century, demonstrated

Army drill from the time of the Napoleonic Wars.

With so many Regimental bands having been disbanded now, it is nostalgic to look back and remember that at the first Berwick Tattoo we welcomed two Scottish Territorial Army bands: the Royal Scots, based in Edinburgh, and the Royal Highland Fusiliers, centred in Glasgow. They gave us a thoroughly Scottish programme, before the Highland Band of the Scottish Division marched on to celebrate the 50th anniversary of the invasion of Normandy and D-Day with a programme of tunes made memorable during that war.

Then we had a complete change of pace as we welcomed the Royal Air Force Police Dog Demonstration Team for their last major display before they disbanded. The move was unpopular with the public and after that handlers and their dogs from RAF stations continued to give displays. 11 years later, a new team was eventually formed at RAF Waddington. Following Edinburgh's lead, the finale piece at that first Tattoo was the now hugely popular Highland Cathedral.

It is important for a Tattoo narrator to be able to see and hear what is going on. It had been difficult to see the first show, so at the second show in 1995 a table and chair and microphone were placed in the entrance to the square. There were members of the public all around me coming and going and curious about what I was doing. It made it hard to concentrate, but there was no value in moaning, so I made the most of it.

The show contained all the expected elements of the pipes and drums and bands from both sides of the Border, including the Northumberland Police Band under the baton of the splendidly named Lieutenant Kevin Crook. We took a nostalgic look back at some of the vehicles which had seen service in the Second World War, the 50th anniversary of which we were marking.

In 1996, we were delighted to welcome the colourful Tara dancers from Lanarkshire, who brought a selection from Riverdance to Berwick Barracks. We were also very pleased to have four Chelsea Pensioners with us for the first time and I had an elevated platform from which I could see the show, but from which it was difficult to communicate.

In 1997, the tattoo programme went into colour inside and we welcomed five pipe bands which made them properly massed on the relatively small Barrack Square. We were also pleased to have the Band of the Brigade of Gurkhas, which always delights a crowd. Playing 'Zorba the Greek' they start slowly and work up to its marching speed of 140 paces to the minute. The Queen's Colour Squadron of the Royal Air Force also put on their immaculate drill display.

In 1998, the Berwick Tattoo stepped up a gear, attracting some of the stars of the Old Moscow Circus with their extraordinary skills and the Central Band of the Royal Air Force, whose Bandmaster and Assistant Conductor, Kenneth Bell, was born in Berwick. In addition to all those, we also managed to bring up from London the opera singer Thora Ker, who had been born and educated in Kelso, not far over the Border in Scotland. We also brought six Chelsea Pensioners on to the Square for the finale and the elderly veterans were given a tremendous reception by the audience.

In the last year of the 20th century, we changed gear again with the young students of the new Army Foundation College training to be the future Senior Non-Commissioned Officers of the Royal Armoured Corps, Royal Artillery and the Infantry. They gave their first major mountain bike display as they worked towards the Festival of Remembrance in the Royal Albert Hall. We also welcomed back more dogs. These were the Dalziel Dog Agility Team from Wishaw in Lanarkshire, pets which run for fun with their owners. They were great fun to work with and entertained the crowd with their antics as they raced around a short course on the Square. Although we made it a competition no-one minded if a dog strayed off course, it was all taken in good part.

For Millennium year, we had a magnificent celebration cake baked for the 100th birthday of Her Majesty Queen Elizabeth the Queen Mother and donated by the British Sugarcraft Guild in a grand raffle. From Kristiansand on the southern coast of Norway, we welcomed the international prize-winning Tveit Union Musikkorps. They played a wonderfully eclectic and highly entertaining programme, which left people asking for them to return.

And in 2001 they did return with other favourites, such as the Edinburgh Tattoo Highland Dancers, more stars from the Old Moscow Circus and the Dalziel Dog Agility Club, as well as some of the Bands who had been stalwarts of the show. To them we added the Ceremony of the Keys from the Tower of London.

We did our best to create at speed an impression of the Tower of London, while an Officer and nine Guardsmen from the Coldstream Guards marched on as the Tower Guard to then be joined by a Sergeant as escort to the Yeoman Warden, Mr Victor Lucas. The Keys have the same symbolic importance to the Tower as a Colour has to a regiment, representing the presence of the sovereign, so they require an escort of a Sergeant and three soldiers, two armed and one unarmed. After going through the steps of the ceremony, where the passage of the keys is checked at various points along the way, 'the Last Post' is played to recall all those who have laid down their lives for their country. The Yeoman Warder returns to report to the Governor of the Tower that all is well, the Crown Jewels are safe and the Ravens are still in the Tower. I had narrated the ceremony at a tattoo in Australia in 2000, so I went to London and talked to the Chief Warder in the Tower on my return. Happily, he agreed that the ceremony could be held in Berwick and I stayed to watch it being carried out in the Tower of London. It was quite a coup for the Tattoo to attract such a ceremony, which bears the mark of 700 years of history and is only rarely seen beyond the grim walls of the old Tower.

But more was to come. I had persuaded the thrilling Russian Cossack State Dance Ensemble from Lipetsk to stay in Scotland after they had appeared at the Edinburgh Tattoo and come to Berwick. They agreed and I hatched a plan for a little extra entertainment using their appearance. There is an old myth which goes back to 1914 and was endorsed by a humorous newspaper article which claimed that Berwick upon Tweed was still at war with Russia, because it had been included in the declaration of the Crimean war, but not in the Peace Treaty. The story was patently nonsense, but many people believed it and Berwick played on it cleverly as great publicity. The bear is the symbol of both Russia and Berwick so I thought that it would be a great idea if the Mayor of Berwick, Councillor Ray Huntley that year, shook hands with the Director of the Moscow Caledonian Club, Vitaly Mironov, before the audience as witnesses to declare the peace official. It was a happy little stunt which went down very well with the audience.

In 2002, we welcomed the Newcastle Nelson Sea Cadet Corps, who brought their quarter-sized field gun – still weighing a quarter of a ton – with them. They carried out the drills of the great Naval Gun races, which commemorated the feat of the Naval Brigade in 1899, when they hauled six guns overland to relieve the Siege of Ladysmith in South Africa. The small gun was broken into seven parts, carried up the Square, reassembled and fired successfully.

Then we celebrated the Golden Jubilee of Her Majesty the Queen, first by recalling the constant raids over the Border by the Border Reivers and then a little re-enactment of the first Queen Elizabeth's great interest in Berwick, as it was she who ordered the construction of the mighty walls which still ring the north and west sides of the town and which remain to this day a marvel of military engineering and a great attraction to visitors. Our present Queen was proclaimed from the steps of the Guildhall in Berwick on 8 February 1952 and the Town Crier Jim Herbert read again the proclamation from the north end of the Barrack Square.

In 2003, the excellent Durham Army Cadet Force Band came north to Berwick for its first appearance at the Tattoo and the students of Queen Victoria School at Dunblane crossed the Border with their pipes, drums and Highland dancers

We re-enacted the visit of King James VI of Scotland, who stopped at Berwick in 1603 on his journey south to also become King James VI of England. He received the homage of the town and was seen off south to the sound of the Border pipes, played by the highly respected Border piper Matt Seattle.

The 2004 Tattoo grew again and we added new guests. Louisa Kelly played the Northumbria Pipes, and one of the Borders' and Scotland's most talented folk singers, Hilary Bell, from Yarrow, asked me to read a couple of verses leading into her first song of nostalgia for the area Borderland. The Adger Drill Band from Norway also performed, as did the quite remarkably athletic singers, dancers and acrobats of the Out of Africa group from Kenya. They were extraordinary, performing on the rough surface of the Square in bare feet without complaints or apparent injury.

In 2005, two groups of young volunteers from the North East of England – the Newcastle Naval Cadets and the Young Fire Fighters of West Denton Fire and Rescue Service in Tyne and

Wear – came to show off their skills in handling fire-fighting equipment. They made an exciting job of handling their kit and I had fun encouraging the audience to urge them on. Three vehicles from the years of the Second World War – two Jeeps and a 15cwt Canadian Chevrolet Signals Truck from 1942 – were brought on to the Square by members of the Lowick Home Guard, who were then joined from the Netherlands by members of the Vereniging Militair Depot from the Netherlands. They were dressed as members of the 7th Battalion of the KOSB who fought at Arnhem, the great airborne battle in the Netherlands, and carried out actions and drills used by British armed forces during the Second World War.

We had worked hard to make Berwick a varied and enjoyable Tattoo, but the prices of equipment, and most particularly the stands, kept rising every year until the costs began to outrun the income. Under charity law in England it was illegal to knowingly spend charity money to make a loss so the members of the Tattoo Trust decided that the 2005 event would have to be last Berwick Tattoo. It was a shame, but at least we had gone out knowing that we had done a good job and entertained a great many people who would not otherwise have been able to see a tattoo.

Happily, it would not be my last tattoo and I had already been doing others at home and abroad.

The Royal Star and Garter Tattoos

In 1999, I was asked to help the Royal Star and Garter Home for disabled ex-servicemen and women with its Tattoos which were aimed at raising money to keep the home going.

The Home then occupied a stunning site on Richmond Hill. This site had originally been the fashionable Star and Garter Hotel, whose splendid conviviality had been enjoyed by every political and artistic personality of the Victoria era, including the writers Charles Dickens, William Makepeace Thackeray and the Poet Laureate Alfred Lord Tennyson. The hotel was killed by the advance of the railway and the motor

WEST BERGHOLT VEHICLE SHOW
AND
COLCHESTER JUBILEE SEARCHLIGHT
TATTOO
2002
in aid of Royal Star & Garter Homes
and local charities
SATURDAY & SUNDAY JULY 27th & 28th
Vehicle show starts 10am both days
Tattoo starts
7pm Saturday

Featuring
RED DEVILS
MUSICAL RIDE OF THE HOUSEHOLD CAVALRY
BAND OF H.M. ROYAL MARINES
BAND OF PARACHUTE REGIMENT
BAND OF ARMY AIR CORPS
BAND OF LIGHT DIVISION
CENTRAL BAND OF ROYAL AIR FORCE
HONDA IMPS MOTOR CYCLE DISPLAY TEAM
ESSEX DOG DISPLAY

car and fell into decay. The Auctioneers and Estate Agents' Institute donated the funds to buy it as a hospital and presented it to Queen Mary, who had expressed her deep concern about the future of the disabled ex-servicemen returning from the War.

There had been little Tattoos run by the Royal Star and Garter before I joined the team, but they seemed to grow in ambition as we went along. The first one I narrated was the fifth West of England Tattoo down at Yeovil Town Football Club's ground at Huish Park on 13 May 1999. It had attracted a high quality cast including the Band of Her Majesty's Royal Marines Commando Training Centre at Lympstone in Devon the Central Band of the Royal Air Force, a display by the Police Dogs from Royal Air Force, Waddington, the Band and Bugles of the Light Division and the beautiful voice of Kelso's Thora Ker singing 'Juliet's Waltz Song', 'the World in Union' and 'Auld Lang Syne' – and it was adventurous to describe a splendid display of team work by the Somerset Fire Brigade Cadets, aged between 12 and 16, as they went along. That was where I first met Simon Weston, the Welsh Guardsman who was horribly burned in the Falklands campaign and who was the Royal Star and Garter's Vice President. He gave a moving address to the crowd and I decided that I would use lines from William Ernest Henley's poem, 'England, My England' to close the show.

Ever the faith endures,
England, my England,
Take us and break
    us: we are yours,
England my own!
...
Chosen daughter
    of the Lord,

The programme for the Royal Star and Garter Show at West Bergholt.

Spouse-in-chief of
the ancient sword,
There's the menace
of the word
In the song on your
bugles blown,
Out of heaven on your
bugles blown!
England – my England

It must have worked, for I was asked back to narrate the first Richmond Grand Military Tattoo at the home of Richmond Rugby Football Club in the shadow of the Royal Star and Garter Home. The Club Rooms had been the home of the Crawdaddy Club, which encouraged the pop music of the 1960s and which was where Mick Jagger and Hot Chocolate had launched their careers. That brought in the Surbiton Youth Band, Police Dogs from the Metropolitan Police, the pipes and drums of the London Irish, the Band and Bugles of the Light Division, a motor cycle display by the young Imps, a musical ride by the Light Cavalry of the Honourable Artillery Company, a ceremonial unit raised and funded by its members to maintain the traditions of mounted military ceremonial, and mounted skill-at-arms wearing uniforms in the authentic style of the Victorian period. Thora Ker returned to sing and Simon Weston spoke before the Royal Star and Garter's volunteer piper Duncan Matthews played 'Sleep, Dearie, Sleep' as the Lone Piper.

Although we had made all the preparations, a year later, the second Grand Richmond Military Tattoo was cancelled and planning began for the rather bigger West Bergholt and Colchester Vehicle and Military Tattoo on Saturday 28 and Sunday 29 July 2001. The Tattoo would be part of an existing military vehicle show being held at West Bergholt, close to the old garrison town of Colchester. We had music from the Bands of the Royal Electrical and Mechanical Engineers and the Hussars and Light Dragoons, gymnastics and comedy from the Kangaroos Gymnastic display team from North Warwickshire, thrilling motor cycle tricks from the Flying Gunners of the Royal Artillery and free fall parachuting displays from the Royal Artillery Parachute Display Team and the Red Devils of the Parachute Regiment.

There was a Jubilee Searchlight Tattoo back at West Bergholt on Saturday 27 July 2002 following a Royal Star and Garter fund-raising concert at Ham House near Richmond the night before. The show was held in the evening and started with a Search and Rescue display by a Sea King helicopter from RAF Wattisham. We enjoyed thrills and comedy from the young Imps motor cycle display team and on four legs the Essex Dog Display Team. The Bands of the Parachute Regiment, the Army Air Corps, the Central Band of the Royal Air Force, the Light Division and Her Majesty's Royal Marines Portsmouth all brought remarkably high quality music to the tattoo, which enjoyed the climax of a classic display of riding and pageantry in the Musical Ride of the Household Cavalry. This was a majestic display to describe and a fine challenge as I had not seen it or described it before, but it thrilled the crowd and I took away an experience which was to bear fruit in future shows.

But even when all the bands and the cast had left the arena, the show was not over. It was dark by now and I had to hold the crowd and build their expectation for a display of night jumping by the Red Devils of the Parachute Regiment. It is really difficult to know precisely when parachutists will leave their aircraft and so I had prepared thorough notes on the history of parachuting; I used a great many of them so that the audience who had stayed had a sound knowledge of the development of parachutes and parachuting from 1783 onwards. When the team left the aircraft the effect was curious. I had often jumped at night as a military parachutist and then our aim was to be as invisible as possible. The Red Devils' jump suits, however, were laced with glow sticks so that at a height they looked like skeletons plunging towards the earth. They all made it safely to the ground to the delight of the crowd who had stayed to watch.

But sadly that tattoo stays in my mind as a tragic event. During one of the Imps' cross-overs, two of the riders' wheels touched. One went down and was run over by the following rider. He was immediately rushed to hospital but after the tattoo we learned that Abbas Malik, a promising 15-year-old, whose confidence had improved greatly since he joined the team, had died. This was the first fatality in the team's history and they were cleared of any failure in care. As it happened, I was looking at my script when the accident occurred, but I suspect that the uneven grass surface most probably led to that split-second delay which caused the slight collision. It was a salutary reminder that in every bold undertaking there is risk. I was honoured to be asked to be the Chairman at the memorial service for Abbas at West Ham United's ground at Upton Park in November.

The following year, the Royal Star and Garter Tattoo moved to the Royal Bath and West Show at Shepton Mallet where we attracted the Central Band of the Royal Air Force, the Hampshire Ex-Servicemen's Band, 93rd (City of Bath) Squadron Band of the Air Training Corps, the Silver Eagles Army Air Corps Free Fall parachute display team, the Royal Signals White Helmets motor cycle display team and the Musical Ride of the Household Cavalry. The Royal Bath and West show ring could easily accommodate all of these magnificent performers with room to spare and the large crowds at the Show crowded round the ring to watch. Earlier, and while the Dropping Zone for the Silver Eagles was being laid out, we enjoyed a short display by the British Army's then newest addition to its battlefield weapons – the Westland WAH-64 tank-busting Apache helicopter, which had peeled off from a test flight to appear at the show.

In 2004, the Band and Bugles of the Light Division opened the tattoo. The Hampshire Ex-Servicemen's band returned to provide the tattoo's music, as did the Adjutant General's Corps and the College Band of the Royal Air Force and the massed pipes and drums from Gordon's Military School, the Surrey Pipe Band from Woking and the locally based Wessex Highlanders. The Royal Signals' White Helmets motor cycle display team returned, the Black Knights Parachute Display team from the Royal Artillery brought well-controlled excitement and the Hampton Court

Horse Rangers Association, a voluntary uniformed youth organisation, performed a series of movements at the trot and canter to the warm appreciation of the big crowds.

The 2005 tattoo was the last one I did for the Royal Star and Garter Home, which had decided to change its fundraising events. In this 60th anniversary year of the ending of the Second World War there was a cornucopia of military music from several of the finest military bands from both sides of the Atlantic, including the Band of the United States' Sixth Fleet based at Naples, Italy, the Plymouth Band of the Royal Marines, the Band and Bugles of the Light Division, the Hampshire Ex-Servicemen's Band and Massed Pipes and Drums. There was the skill and grace of superb horsemanship from the Household Cavalry and some hair-raising action from the motor cyclists of the Royal Signals White Helmets Display Team. In the 200th anniversary year of victory at the Battle of Trafalgar, the sky-diving parachutists of the Royal Navy Raiders Parachute Display Team also performed.

All of these tattoos were addressed by Simon Weston and it was a pleasure to work with him to raise money for this most worthy establishment for rehabilitating veterans.

Traquair

I usually have to travel some distance to present a tattoo, sometimes half way round the world, but there was a series of small biennial tattoos promoted by the St Ronan's Silver Band at the historic Traquair House, near the town of Innerleithen at the western end of the Scottish Borders. St Ronan's Silver Band, which claims to be the oldest band of its kind in Scotland, has a very strong record in the brass band

THE ST. RONAN'S
TATTOO

Innerleithen **TRAQUAIR HOUSE** Scottish Borders

Celebrate the Golden Jubilee

with the Music of the Commonwealth

SUNDAY 2 JUNE 2002

www.stronanstattoo.org
Souvenir Programme £1

The programme for the Golden Jubilee Tattoo at Traquair House.

world and was able to attract the Royal British Legion Scotland Band to its first Tattoo in 2000. Pipe bands from Innerleithen, Selkirk and Barnton provided a contrast to the brass bands from St Ronan's, Peebles and Selkirk.

Traquair was a favourite house for the old Scottish kings to do business and to relax, being close to the hunting ground of Ettrick Forest which abounded with bears and wolves, deer, wild cat and boar. So, to remember Traquair's royal favour, a drama group from Borders Youth Theatre re-enacted the granting of the charter to Glasgow by William the Lion and I had real pleasure in writing a crisp history of Scotland as the thread of the narration for this Tattoo right up to the departure in 1745 of Bonnie Prince Charlie through the Bear Gates at the end of the long grass drive on which the Tattoo was held. The gates have remained shut ever since, awaiting the return of a Stewart monarch.

Music of the Commonwealth for the Queen's Golden Jubilee in 2002 was played by St Ronan's Silver Band with Selkirk Silver Band and pipe bands from Innerleithen and the Scottish Ambulance Service and the Black Star Steel Band from Glasgow.

The bands which accepted the invitation from St Ronan's Silver Band to appear in the 2004 tattoo were Jedforest Instrumental Band from Jedburgh, the West Lothian Schools Brass Band, the Innerleithen Pipe Band and Edinburgh Postal Pipe Band.

The 2006 tattoo at Traquair took on an international mantle with the visit of the Dutch Showbrass Band Thalita in their British-style uniforms who played a Latin American piece from the American composer Carmine Pastores. With them were St Ronan's Silver Band and Selkirk Silver Band and the Innerleithen Pipe Band and Edinburgh Postal Service Pipe Band

2008 saw the final tattoo at Traquair in the capable hands of the Director of Music Alex Knox. Under his baton St Ronan's Silver Band and Peebles Burgh Silver Band, Innerleithen Pipe Band and George Watson's Juvenile Pipe Band gave the audience an entertaining afternoon of mainly Scottish music in the lovely Border setting.

Inverness

In 2007 the Inverness Tattoo was moved from the Northern Meeting Park in Inverness, where it had been held for the last 55 years, to the historic Fort George Barracks 14 miles away as part of the Highland 2007 celebrations of Highland culture. I had the pleasant task of narrating the show in tandem with John Harrison whose voice usually described the tattoo in Inverness. The show opened with a parachuting display by the Golden Lions Freefall Parachute Display Team representing the seven Battalions of the Royal Regiment of Scotland. There were pipe bands from the Royal Scots Dragoon Guards, the Black Watch battalion of the Royal Regiment of Scotland, the Royal British Legion Scotland and the Royal Army of Oman led by Pipe Major Derek Potter of the SCOTS DG, a future Queen's Piper, and Drum Major Brian Alexander of the Black Watch

The marvellous Imps motorcycle display team travelled all the way from East London to give the crowd an exciting display of tricks spiced with a little humour.

The Edinburgh Tattoo

Ceilidh Dancers brought their exciting Ceilidh Dance to Fort George and the Pipers and Drummers of the Royal Army of Oman returned to Scotland to pay their tribute from an old British ally to Highland culture. We also had three superb military bands the Royal Regiment of Scotland, the Northern Band of the Royal Signals and the Lowland Band of the Royal Regiment of Scotland which added their music to make this a memorable celebration of Highland culture.

Durham

When the military organisations in the North East of England decided that they would like to stage a Tattoo in 2008 to mark the Centenary of the Territorial Army I was enormously flattered to be asked to come and narrate it. It was to be held on Palace Green on the grass arena outside Durham's magnificent Norman Cathedral, which allowed for a compact area inside the stands built for the spectators.

The Territorial Army or the Territorial Force as it was first known was created in 1908 from the groups of Volunteers

The Durham Tattoo, celebrating the centenary of the Territorial Army in 2008.

Territorial Army Centenary Celebration

DURHAM TATTOO

Palace Green
Saturday 6th September 2008
Evening Performance

which had existed in one form or another long before that. The perception of its members as amateurish weekend soldiers had been exploded with TA soldiers already deploying on operations alongside Regular troops. In 2008, 1,500 Territorial soldiers would be deployed on operations, eight per cent of the Army in action. Over 15,000 Territorials had already served on operations in Iraq and Afghanistan, with some losing their lives and others returning wounded. Honouring their service was a debt we owed them.

Having served 32 years in the Territorial Army, 22 years in the Parachute Regiment and ten with the Central

Volunteer Headquarters, it was a relatively straightforward task to write a script for the Tattoo which first told the story of the First World War into which many members of the Territorial Force marched willingly and was brought to life on the arena by members of the Great War Society. That was followed by a Second World War re-enactment of a raid by airborne troops on a German fuel dump. Winston Churchill in the person of Paul Hilditch recreated his speech in Fulton, Missouri describing the division of Europe after the war. Then another enactment of contemporary action with a combined patrol of Territorial and Regular troops coming under fire and dealing with their attackers. The Tattoo showed Naval Reserves and a skills competition between local Army Cadet Force units. There was music too to spice the action from the Royal Signals Northern Band, the Royal Regiment of Fusiliers, the Durham ACF Borneo Band, three pipe bands and the bright singing talent of 17-year-old Amy Holford.

This was a different style of tattoo, relying on a lot more narration to tell the audience what the action represented, so it was a concentrated and rewarding task for a writer and narrator. Planning had started more than two years earlier which meant regular visits to Durham, but none of that could plan for the heavy rain which beset the country that weekend. By a marvellous turn of fortune the rain which had dogged the afternoon rehearsal cleared just before the evening performance. But after the show driving back to the Scottish Borders from Durham was as big an adventure as the show with the A1 blocked by flood water north of Newcastle, deep water in the centre of Ponteland on the alternative route and, having navigated that, stretches of deep water lying in wait across the Northumberland moors in the dark.

Buxton

At the start of 2010 a group of enthusiastic volunteers had decided to raise money for the ABF – The Soldiers' Charity by holding a Tattoo in the magnificent Dome in the spa town of Buxton high in the Derbyshire hills during the town's annual arts festival. They generously asked me if I would provide the script and narration which I readily agreed to do, although the commitment would be concentrated into one day, with rehearsals on a Saturday morning and two performances in the afternoon and evening. It was hard work but the Buxton Tattoo is still going

The Dome was originally a stable block commissioned by the Duke of Devonshire in 1779 and in 1882 the huge Dome, then the largest in the world, was added to create a hospital. Now the building is part of the University of Derby. Although there is room for less than 1,000 people and

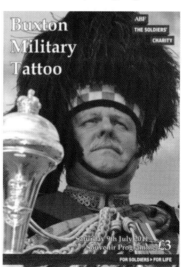

A brand new Tattoo was started in the Peak District of Derbyshire in 2010.

The remarkable Dome in Buxton.

the acoustics are difficult the show has proved remarkably popular with a mixture of local and national bands appearing over the years. The first show attracted the Heavy Cavalry and Cambrai Band from Catterick with Gary Chilton of The Soldiers singing trio, the Volunteer Band of the Mercian Regiment and the ACF Derbyshire Band along with the Regimental Ram mascot Private Derby the 29th, the Pipes and Drums of RAF Waddington, the volunteer Nottinghamshire Band of the Royal Engineers, the crisp efficiency of 126 (City of Derby) Squadron of the Air Training Corps Weapons Drill Display Team and an inter service Cadet Light Gun race. I had the pleasure of researching, writing and narrating a tribute on the centenary of Derbyshire's Florence Nightingale and learning more about the life of this remarkable woman who in the 19th century was the most famous woman in the Empire after Queen Victoria.

In 2011 some of the same performers returned and we added the Lancashire Artillery Volunteer Band and the Yorkshire Volunteers Band to the roll of Buxton performers. The following year the audience was treated to the local percussion skills of the Corps of Drums of 2517 (Buxton) Squadron of the Air Cadets, the singing of the Rolls Royce Male Voice and Ladies Choirs, the Pipes and Drums of the Manchester Branch of the Scots Guards Association, the Regimental Band of the Duke of Lancaster's Regiment and the Band of the King's Division. The Buxton Tattoo was proving to be a wonderful showcase for young and volunteer bands and in

2013 the Band of 366 (King Ecgbert) Squadron of the RAF Air Cadets and the Territorial Army Band of the Royal Welsh Regiment took to the floor, along with the Waterloo Band and Bugles of the Rifles, the Band of the Corps of Royal Engineers and the Drums and Pipes of the First Battalion Irish Guards. Serving soldiers from the Second Battalion of the Mercian Regiment demonstrated the military skills they were using in the field in Afghanistan as a useful reminder that soldiering is not only about parading in smart uniforms.

Many of the performers were happy to return regularly and in 2014 the Royal Signals Northern Band joined the roll of participants at Buxton along with the Pipes and Drums of the First Battalion the Royal Regiment of Scotland the Royal Scots Borderers and the Band of the Irish Guards. The following year, the Pipes and Drums of the Royal Dragoon Guards and the Band of the Royal Armoured Corps joined the list and with it came its Forward Operating Base Rock Team.

Since around 2010 one of the roles of Army bands has been to bring moral support to the lads on the front line. While the RAC Band was in Afghanistan some of its members formed a small Rock Team which went out to entertain troops at the sharp end in their Forward Operating Bases from which tactical operations could be mounted quickly against enemy threats. The Rock Team's instruments and other kit could fit into a small all-terrain-vehicle and trailer and would be helicoptered forward from their Main Operating Base in a Chinook to bring a bit of cheer from home to the lads operating close to the enemy. It was a pleasure to be able to describe in a Tattoo some of the tasks which our forces, including their musicians, are ready to undertake even under combat conditions.

Dover
To mark the historic milestone of the Queen's Jubilee Year in 2012, a number of places chose to present Tattoos. In Dover, from where Admiral Sir Bertram Ramsay planned the miraculous evacuation from Dunkirk in 1940 and commanded the naval part

in the invasion of France
on D-Day in 1944, a tattoo
was held at Connaught
Barracks in Fort Burgoyne.

The evening show opened
with a parachute display from
the Tigers, the flagship team of
the Princess of Wales's Royal
Regiment, the senior English
Infantry Regiment of the line.
The parachutists were jumping
on to the tarmac arena and a
guest parachutist from another
unit landed awkwardly
injuring himself very seriously.
The show had to wait while
the medical team assessed him
and then began the delicate
task to taking him for hospital
treatment. I had taken the
decision not to carry with me
the long notes on the history
of parachuting which I had
used at West Bergholt while
we waited for the Red Devils
in 2002, so I had to think very
quickly about how to fill an
indeterminate time while the
unfortunate parachutist was
being treated in the full gaze
of the shocked public. It was
one of those awful tests which
you do not expect and which
I had stupidly decided would
be unlikely to happen given all
the drops I had witnessed and
described during the previous
20 years. I should have known

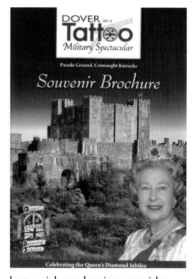

but, without having any idea
of how long the medical
treatment of the injured man
was going to take on the arena,
I reached into my experience
as a volunteer parachutist
in the Scottish TA Battalion
of the Parachute Regiment
for 22 years. To hold the
audience's attention I started
to describe the techniques for
military parachuting and the
differences between those and
the free-fall jumping which
the audience had just been
watching. I described them
in great detail and although
I cannot remember exactly
what I said, seem to recall
that I was flowing nicely
when the ambulance bore
the unfortunate jumper away

THE GREATEST SHOW ON EARTH

and we were able to start the tattoo. Some long-standing friends had come over from Canterbury to watch the event and were kind enough to say that they had found it all rather interesting.

Thankfully, the rest of the Tattoo passed off without any further hazards. The fanfare trumpeters of the Adjutant General's Corps and the Army Air Corps opened with the well named Diamond Jubilee. We enjoyed the music of the Kent Massed Sea Cadet Bands, The Band of the Princess of Wales's Royal Regiment TA and the Band of the Brigade of Gurkhas along with their Pipes and Drums and dancers with their kukri knife display. The Tonbridge Combined Cadet Force represented all three services with its silent drill display, members of the Third Battalion PWRR TA demonstrated what the modern infantry soldier had to face on the modern battlefield, the Royal Signals White Helmets motor cycle display team took everyone's minds off the earlier accident with a thrilling display before the lead singer of The Soldiers trio, WOII Gary Chilton sang Amazing Grace and asked the audience to join in the last verse. To close the Tattoo in Dover I chose lines from the stirring poem 'Ye Mariners of England' written at the start of the 19th century by the Scottish poet Thomas Campbell whose name is hardly remembered now but was famous in his day. He was buried in Westminster Abbey and has a statue on the south side of George Square in Glasgow, a long way north of the white cliffs of Dover.

Britannia needs no bulwarks,
No towers along the steep;
Her march is o'er the
mountain-waves,
Her home is on the deep.
Then, then, ye
ocean-warriors!
Our song and feast shall flow
When the fiery fight
is heard no more,
And the storm has
ceased to blow.

The Dover Tattoo had been held on the weekend of the Thames Diamond Jubilee Pageant, in which a flotilla of 670 vessels made its way from Wandsworth to Tower Bridge, joined by the Royal Barge 'Spirit of Chartwell' bearing Her Majesty, Prince Philip, Prince Charles, the

Duchess of Cornwall, Prince
William, the Duchess of
Cambridge and Prince Harry.
Concentrating on the Tattoo,
I had not bargained for a
really difficult, slow and very
crowded journey into London
as huge numbers of people
converged on the centre of the
city to watch the Pageant.

Northeast Lincolnshire

Three weeks later the people
of Cleethorpes in North
East Lincolnshire held a
Diamond Jubilee Tattoo in
the Meridian Park Arena
in Cleethorpes. The people
of the town are known as
Meggies. How it came about
is open to speculation. I
prefer the theory that it has
its origins in the military
history of Lincolnshire, when
the local commandant of the
1st Volunteer Battalion of the
Lincolnshire Regiment was
Captain HW Meggitt and
the unit adopted the term
Meggie to distinguish them
from the Yellowbellies of the
Lincolnshire Fens. This was a
part of the world I had never
visited so it was as much out
of curiosity as a willingness
to help that I undertook the
show. The weather during
the day was mixed and the

forecast for the evening had
been poor which probably
kept many people away. As it
turned out, the weather was
not as bad as we had expected
and the Band of the Royal
Air Force College opened
the show with the fanfare
Shining Sword composed
by Wing Commander
Rob Wiffin as a tribute to
the heroism of the men of
wartime Bomber Command,
many of whom flew from
bases in Lincolnshire. 'The
shining sword' was how Sir
Arthur Harris described
the Lancaster bomber.

   In William Shakespeare's
play *King Henry the Fourth*,
Sir John Falstaff tells the

King he is as melancholy as the drone of a Lincolnshire bagpipe, but the pipes and drums of the Lincolnshire-based Royal Air Force Waddington were certainly not melancholy as they played a cheerful set followed by the Band of the Brigade of Gurkhas with their kukri knife wielding dancers. The original Military Wives Choir based in Catterick Garrison in North Yorkshire was joined by the choir from Dishforth for a set of the favourite songs recorded by Military Wives Choirs. I had been a little surprised before the show when one of the singers asked me if I had any experience of presenting events. I thought that the kindest and most diplomatic answer was simply 'yes'. The Humberside Police Band was followed by the Police Dog Section and PC Richard Brock and Police Dog Louis who dealt with 'an intruder' who ran on to the arena to disrupt the show. These little diversions are always fun to narrate since they are always fluid and appeal to the crowd. The Royal Signals White Helmets gave another thrilling, high-speed display doing wheelies out of the arena and I chose a verse from the Knights of Arnhem by the Scottish Border poet Will Ogilvie to introduce the evening hymn, returning to England My England to round off the show.

Tyne and Wear

A week later the North East of England united for a Tyne and Wear Diamond Jubilee Tattoo at the University of Sunderland. We squeezed in a matinee performance, which acted as a dress rehearsal, before the evening show. I noted how much Britain has changed over the previous 60 years. In the 1950s British soldiers were in action in Korea, Teddy Boys walked the streets, high overhead the space race was beginning and teenagers were discovering rock and roll. So we started with the skill and enthusiasm of the nation's youth represented by the Band and Bugles of the Durham Army Cadet Force. The Pipes and Drums of the Royal Electrical and Mechanical Engineers played a set before they were joined by the Highland dancers from the local Scott and Whistler Schools of Highland Dancing. Local members of the three

The Diamond
Jubilee Tattoo
in Sunderland.

cadet services Army, Sea and
Air, went head to head in
a challenge to see which of
them would be first to erect
a nine feet by nine Army tent
and then get over a portable
climbing wall. I always enjoy
these little events when I can
encourage the audience to
get involved in cheering on
the team they want to win.
Ryhope, south of Sunderland,
was first a farming community
before it turned to coal
mining. The Ryhope Allstars,
with members ranging from
four years old to 50-plus,
played with all the razzmatazz
of an American-style marching
band before the North East
Hindu Cultural Trust brought
the sound and the colour of the

Commonwealth to the arena.
We raced through an amusing
glance back over the music
and action of the Queen's 60
years on the throne. With
pop music playing, and re-
enactors and vehicles on the
arena, I had great fun reading
the history I had written of
the period in the North East.
It had to move swiftly to
hold the audience's attention
but not so fast it outran the
music and the performers.
It seemed to work and the
Heavy Cavalry and Cambrai
Band cast our minds forward
a month to the opening of the
Olympic Games in London.
The show ended in the style of
the Last Night of the Proms
with singers Julie Pendleton
and John Rowland arriving in
a Second World War Austin
Tilly to lead the audience in
'Jerusalem', 'Land of Hope and
Glory' and 'Rule Britannia'.

I am sure Her Majesty
would have been proud
of the loyalty shown up
and down the country by
all these demonstrations
of Jubilee affection.

Fort George
The Inverness Tattoo
eventually folded its tents after
its Golden Jubilee in 2011 but

it was much missed and Major General Seymour Monro, a former commander of the Queen's Own Highlanders before becoming Deputy Commander of the NATO Rapid Reaction Corps, was determined that it should not slip away without a fight. He decided that he would use the historic barracks at Fort George as the setting for a Highland Tattoo and in 2014 an international cast gathered under the producer, Major Bruce Hitchings, a former Queen's Own Highlander Pipe Major and former Senior Pipe Major of the British Army. Once again I had the able assistance of the man who had described most of the Inverness Tattoos, Captain John Harrison.

Before the show, there was a marvellous display of flying by Neil Geddes in one of the early World War One aircraft, a Scout Experimental Five SE5A aircraft introduced into service with the Royal Flying Corps in 1917.

Once the show itself got under way we had a wonderful mix of music, action and drama with music from the Pipers and drummers from the Black Watch and the Highlanders, the Third and Fourth Battalions of the Royal Regiment of Scotland, RAF Lossiemouth, 2622 Squadron Royal Auxiliary Air Force, Forres, Gordonstoun School, Highland Army Cadet Force and City of Inverness Youth, all drilled by Major Hitchings and one of the world's leading solo pipers, Pipe Major Robert Watt from Maghera in Northern Ireland. There were the young musicians of the Fochabers Fiddlers who had been making a reputation around the Highlands and Moray for the quality of their playing and the Band of the Royal Regiment of Scotland with one of their musicians, Lance Corporal Alan Bell singing the Green Fields of France, a song set in the aftermath of the four and a half month long Battle of the Somme in 1916.

West Point, overlooking the Hudson River, is the United States of America's Officer training Academy and the fifers and drummers who provide the music for the Academy have become known as the Hellcats because of their task of waking the Corps of Cadets early in the morning. I had first heard the Hellcats

The Highland
Military Tattoo
at Fort George.

The
HIGHLAND
MILITARY
TATTOO

OFFICIAL PROGRAMME

Friday 5th to Sunday 7th September 2014

£4

at the Stone Mountain Tattoo in 1993 and again in New York earlier in 2014. With their different style to British Bands they were a dramatic contrast to any of the other performers and were very much appreciated by the Highland crowd. I was made an honorary Hellcat after narrating their show in New York and again at Fort George and I treasure the carefully folded and cased American flag with which I was presented by them as a unique memento of our association.

Dancers from among the serving soldiers of the Black Watch Third Battalion the Royal Regiment of Scotland, stationed at Fort George,

gave a superb demonstration of the traditional sword dance, said to have been a warrior's dance of triumph after a successful battle, and were followed by the young ladies of the Ailsa Craig Dancers with Broadswords where four swords were laid tip to tip to form a cross.

A little competition is guaranteed to get the audience keenly involved and we staged a 'gun race' between two teams from the Army's 39 Engineer Regiment based at Kinloss. They were not handling real guns but the elements which the teams needed to carry were pretty heavy just the same, logs, barrels, jerry cans, ammunition boxes and large and small tyres weighing around 200 kilogrammes altogether. The audience got into the spirit of the competition roaring on the teams over four nights

There were two historical vignettes. The first portrayed the Battle of Culloden in 1746 and the Jacobite insurrection which led to the building of Fort George and was brought to a moving close by Fiona Mackenzie singing in Gaelic the Lament for William Chisholm who was killed in the Jacobite Army at Culloden. Careful co-ordination between the script and the action on the arena took a little while but it all worked well on the night. The second vignette was witty as well as poignant and writing and narrating the script for that was a little easier. It portrayed the recruiting of volunteers to go off from the Highlands to the First World War, the centenary of which we were remembering that year.

Sensibly the Army used the occasion as an ideal parade on which to present Long Service and Good Conduct Medals to four soldiers and a Long Service and Good Conduct Medal and the Accumulated Campaign Service Medal to a fifth, and the evening was brought to a resounding end with a magnificent display of fireworks.

The first Highland Tattoo was a resounding success and led to demands for another the following year so in 2015 Flypasts by Typhoon FGR4 aircraft opened each show bang on time.

I flew solo for this Tattoo and once again the massed pipes and drums opened with General Seymour Monro's Welcome. They took us into the first of that year's vignettes marking the 200th anniversary of the Duke of Wellington's success at the Battle of Waterloo. I did a lot of research and tried to compress a long day's battle and the lead up to it into a few comprehensible minutes. For this we had horses, cannon and Highland soldiers in squares. We managed to portray the action of the Sergeant Charles Ewart capturing the eagle of the French 45th Regiment and the Senior Pipe Major of the British Army, WO1 Martin Macdonald, played the role of Piper Kenneth Mackay of the 79th Cameron Highlanders who stepped outside his square and, playing a famous Highland tune War or Peace, rallied his colleagues to the astonishment of the French. By a happy chance, WO1 Macdonald was born only a few miles from the home of Piper Mackay on the north coast of Scotland.

The second vignette portrayed a couple of the actions of Scottish soldiers in the First World War, Piper Daniel Laidlaw winning the Victoria Cross at the Battle of Loos and the inspired action of Lieutenant Philip Christison of the Queen's Own Cameron Highlanders, who sang in Gaelic the stirring 'March of the Cameron Men' to encourage his Cameron men to follow him to help retake Hill 70. Lieutenant Christison became General Sir Philip Christison who played a significant part in the defeat of the Japanese in the Far East in the Second World War and in the early establishment of the Edinburgh Tattoo. Writing and then narrating these vignettes along with the action makes the Tattoo a lot more interesting.

The City of Inverness Highland Dancers and the City of Inverness Contemporary Dance Group graced the Tattoo with traditional and modern Highland dancing and the talented young musicians from the Highland Youth Ceilidh Band, 'snas, Gaelic for cool, played Highland music.

Making the Tattoo international once again was the Stadacona Band which has been a mainstay in the Maritime military community on the East Coast of Canada for over 70 years and is often referred to as 'the finest band in the land.' Their entertaining set included a pipe solo by Warrant Officer Katherine Buckland playing the Flying Saucer Reel.

Then the Band of the Royal Artillery took us to an inter-services competition between Royal Marine Commandos, the Army's 39 Engineer Regiment and 51 Squadron of the RAF Regiment. They had to move nine whisky barrels up and down the arena which included crossing a deep trench. This was a test which needed strength and ingenuity and was eventually won after five runs by the Army, who carried off six bottles of Glenmorangie whisky. Trying to encourage the audience and the teams is fun and brings the audience much closer to being part of the show.

More fireworks lit up the night sky to round off another memorable display at the historic barracks.

Other Tattoos Overseas

THE GREAT TATTOO in Edinburgh is the gold standard and it has opened the doors to many other tattoos around the world. Music is a universal language and the players who have performed at Edinburgh will be welcomed anywhere. Narrating is not quite so universal and I have only once managed to penetrate a country whose native language was not English but I have had the pleasure of writing and narrating a wonderful variety of tattoos in several countries

1993 Stone Mountain, Georgia, USA

When you watch the Edinburgh Tattoo night after night you might think you were spoiled for anything else, but in mid-October 1993 I had the pleasure of commentating at the annual tattoo which precedes the Stone Mountain Highland Games just outside Atlanta in the deep south of the United States of America.

People there have a fierce pride in their Scottish heritage and every year thousands gather at the foot of the extraordinary granite mound which rises from the flat plain east of the Georgian city to celebrate.

They start with a tattoo which gathers together pipe bands from up and down North America and overseas. It is certainly different from Edinburgh but no less fun. Most obviously it does not have the incomparable backdrop of Edinburgh's old castle; it is held in a covered horse-jumping arena with an earthen floor, but the spirit is every bit as keen as it is in Scotland.

That year's Stone Mountain Tattoo boasted five pipe bands. The 1st Battalion, King's Own Scottish Borderers brought the authentic air of Scotland with them, there were two pipe bands from Toronto, the 48th Highlanders of Canada and the Metropolitan Toronto

Police Pipes and Drums while Atlanta produced the other two, the championship winning Atlanta Pipe Band and the John Mohr Mackintosh Pipes and Drums.

The pipes and drums were joined by military bands from both sides of the North American border – The Hellcats, the buglers and drummers of the United States Military Academy at West Point, the Army Ground Forces Band from Fort McPherson in Atlanta and the Band of the Royal Regiment of Canada from Toronto.

Stone Mountain had its answer to the dancers at Edinburgh with Highland dancers from Toronto and Country dancers from Atlanta and the popular Alex Beaton, who had left Scotland 30 years earlier to settle in America, led the crowd in many of the songs which Scots seem to be born knowing and never forget wherever they may wander.

With a programme which lasted for nearly three hours the sell-out audience of more than 4,000 people from all over the United States got good value for their money. Marching and counter-marching, singly and together

the bands played all the traditional favourite tunes, although for me the sound of the KOSB band playing 'Blue Bonnets o'er the Border' had a special poignancy. It was one of the tunes played by Piper Daniel Laidlaw when he won his Victoria Cross at the Battle of Loos in 1915 and the pipes he played then were being played by Private Kevin Turnbull from Selkirk in the band at Stone Mountain. History must be vibrant to catch the imagination and here was the most remarkable historical bridge spanning more than 75 years, from the hell of war in northern France, through the ancient traditions of the Scottish Borders. The knowledge helped to bring the traditions of the 300-year-old Regiment to life for an audience whose history may be more easily measured in decades rather than centuries.

So too did the presence at the tattoo of the Honoured Guest, Sir Lachlan Maclean of Duart and Morvern, Chief of a clan which claims descent from the fifth century. He was presented with a specially carved cromach as a permanent reminder of his visit to Stone Mountain and the many Scots over the water.

Americans may sometimes give the impression of bringing Brigadoon to life, but there is no doubting the passionate sincerity of their attachment to Scotland and the traditions which it has given the world. While they remain so strongly linked to the land of their fathers Scotland will always be the spiritual home of many more people than could ever hope to crowd within her borders.

1995 Springfield, Massachusetts

Two years later, on 16 and 17 June 1995, I was back in America for a rather different tattoo held in the shadow of the historic Springfield Armory in Massachusetts. This one was much smaller than the Stone Mountain event and run by people in the Springfield Technical Community College who realised that a tattoo was a great idea but had not the experience to know how much work and expense was involved in creating a good show.

Springfield Armory is one of America's most historic sites and is now in the care of the National Park Service.

Two hundred years earlier, President George Washington had approved the site as the location of the young nation's first arsenal because of its obvious geographical advantages in the northern theatre of war lying at the intersection of three rivers and four major roads and located just north of the Connecticut River's first waterfall which is too steep to be navigated by ocean-going vessels. Springfield was therefore the first town on the Connecticut River protected from attack by seafaring naval vessels and sufficiently far inland to be safe from the British coastal raiding parties.

Until 1968, Springfield Armory was the centre for the research, development and manufacture of American small arms. The legendary Springfield rifle and the Second World War workhorse, the M1 Garand rifle, were made there. At the height of production during the Second World 5000 M1s a day were being turned out of the buildings which were the backdrop for the tattoo.

The Springfield Tattoo was just one part of a much larger Outdoor Festival and Game

Fair being held at Springfield and at the nearby Westover Air Reserve Base at Chicopee and was small by comparison with most tattoos, with the Lowland Band of the Scottish Division which had flown in from Scotland, the local Melha Highlanders pipe band from Springfield and the Middlesex County Volunteer Fifes and Drums from the Boston area of Massachusetts.

I had great difficulty being paid the cost of the flight out to America but in the end the organisers came through and the job was done. I was able to invite old friends from nearby to come and enjoy the show so there were compensations as well as pressures to make it a worthwhile trip.

The audience was small and sat on small bleachers (stands) as each act performed twice before the show was brought to a fine close by the Lowland Band from Edinburgh playing 'Amazing Grace' led off by Pipe Major Alastair McIntosh.

One of the continuing challenges in writing an appropriate script is to know quite how to finish it. Sir Walter Scott's stirring words which finish Edinburgh are not quite right everywhere,

but happily Henry Wadsworth Longfellow had written a long poem as a paean to the Arsenal at Springfield and I took the first and last verses from that to bring the show to a close.

> This is the Arsenal
> from floor to ceiling
> Like a huge organ rise
> the burnished arms
> But from their silent pipes
> no anthem pealing
> Startles the villages
> with strange alarms.

> Peace! and no longer
> from its brazen portals
> The blast of war's great
> organ shakes the skies
> But beautiful as songs
> of the immortals
> The holy melodies
> of love arise.

Now that the old buildings had become an ivy-clad museum featuring the world's largest collection of historic American firearms and no longer turning out weapons, it felt as though Longfellow's lines had been prophetic and were now appropriate because they were true.

1996 Brisbane, Queensland

On 23 May 1996, Pixie Campbell, Michael Parker's superbly efficient tattoo assistant, had very kindly asked me to dinner to meet Lieutenant Colonel Colin Harper and his wife Wendy who were in Scotland on a nostalgic visit from Australia. Colin had been a bandmaster with the Gordon Highlanders before he moved to Australia and rose to the rank of Lieutenant Colonel as Senior Director of Music for the Australian Army. After he retired, he immediately began to promote popular concerts in Brisbane in his wife's home state of Queensland.

Colin was preparing a tattoo in Brisbane and as it happened I had gone there from Scotland at the age of 14 and spent a year at Brisbane State High School before starting work in a commercial radio station in Brisbane. We agreed that as soon as Edinburgh was over that year I would race out to Brisbane to present the first of what would be three Tattoos that I would narrate for Colin in Brisbane.

This tattoo, with its strong international influence, would be just one of more than 100

The first Brisbane International Tattoo.

events taking place at the Brisbane Festival and would be held indoors in the Great Hall of the Brisbane Exhibition and Conference Centre. I wondered why it was being held indoors in a sub-tropical city until the Festival Cavalcade was cancelled because of the monsoon rain which lashed the city the day before the show.

Unlike Edinburgh, Colin opened his Tattoo with the huge sound of the Bands of the Grenadier Guards, the Australian Army Brisbane, Royal Military College at Duntroon, South Australia Police, New Zealand Army and Royal Brunei Armed Forces which set the scene for the band of the Royal

Australian Navy and then the Thula Sizwe Zulus from South Africa with their traditional Mbube War Dance. The Band of the South Australia Police led to the Massed Pipes and Drums of the 9th Battalion the Royal Queensland Regiment, the Queensland Irish Association, the St Andrews Pipe Band Brisbane and the Queensland Police who played for the Highland dancers from southern Queensland and northern New South Wales, co-ordinated by Margaret Paterson. Then I had the first experience of the New Zealand Army Band with its nine minutes of non-stop energy. It was after that Tattoo that I told the Producer in Edinburgh I was sure that the Band would be a huge hit in Edinburgh as it has proved on all its appearances since.

This Brisbane Tattoo had an interval, as all the locally produced Tattoos have had in Australia. The Band of the Grenadier Guards opened the second half with a tune commemorating the Battle Honour won by the Regiment in the Gulf War, 'Wadi al Batin', before the band broke into a medley of British tunes. The Band proved that it was a good sport as it stayed on to play 'The Parade of the Wooden Soldiers', which brought out the young Davidia Lind dancers all dressed as Guardsmen. They paraded wonderfully well but I am sure their drill would have made an RSM weep. As a stern contrast the Queen's Colour Squadron of the Royal Air Force carried out its skilled, precision drill display. The Royal Brunei Armed Forces Band and the Pipes and Drums of the Royal Brunei Land Forces played a couple of local fishermen's songs before the Finale which flowed on entirely traditional lines.

It was a most enjoyable way to return to the city where I finished my schooling but there was one puzzle. I had been placed in a soundproof booth for the narration but it was so soundproof that I could hear virtually nothing of the show and had to watch the audience's hands to tell me when I should introduce the next act. I asked that if I was asked to narrate the next show I would like to sit in the arena between the sound desk and the stage manager.

1998 Brisbane

Happily I was asked back to Brisbane and did indeed sit where I had requested. This time the Hall had been extended with temporary stands erected in the extra area.

Once again Colin started with a big sound. The Band of Her Majesty's Royal Marines Portsmouth, the Russian Army Central Band, the New Zealand Army Band and the Band of the Royal Army of Oman marched on to 'Buffalo Hunt' from *Dances with Wolves*, then gave way to another group new to me from those Polynesian islands which gave the world the name and the practice of body marking which are also called tattoos. This was the Royal Corps of Musicians of the Tonga Defence Services and their Music Director Captain the Hon Ve'ehala who had raised and trained the Band. They played a programme similar to the style of the New Zealand Army Band, but with a distinctly South Pacific flavour bringing out male 'warriors' with traditional Tongan war dances, and then the ladies displayed the graceful Tau'olunga

THE 1998 ENERGEX BRISBANE FESTIVAL
in association with CHANNEL 9
presents the
INTERNATIONAL TATTOO

The 1998 Brisbane Tattoo programme.

dancing, the traditional way to entertain a chief, with hand movements illustrating the song. As soon as I got back to Scotland I recommended to the Producer in Edinburgh that we should bring them to Scotland and happily they have been several times since and were with us in Melbourne and Wellington in 2016. The Band of Her Majesty's Royal Marines played and displayed with all their world renowned skill before the Band of the Royal Army of Oman played a well judged mixture of Omani and western music.

During the Omani Band's performance the Stage Manager received word that one of the temporary stands had started to buckle so we had to make very quick decisions. The Producer forbade us to stop the show but the Stage Manager rightly overruled him and as soon as the Omanis left the arena I announced the interval and asked the people sitting in the collapsing stand to come down on to the arena, I did not tell them why and I guess the tone of voice must have reassured them for no-one started rushing. The stewards helped to shepherd them all down and no-one was any the wiser until the stand was clear and then I explained that because it had started to collapse we could not let them return. The morning paper *The Courier Mail* made a small reference to the incident the next day but since no-one had been hurt it did not have a sensational story to splash. Back in the hall a decision was made to offer people the alternatives of their money back, tickets for a future performance, the chance to take one of the few unoccupied seats in the rest of the stands or collect a chair and sit around the arena. I could not believe my eyes when the people who had decided to take the last

option placed their chairs inside the safety barrier around the arena. So before we could continue I had to ask them to move behind the barrier.

We started again with Highland and Irish dancing and the Central Band of the Russian Army under its Chief Conductor and Inspector of Military Bands in the Russian Federation, Lieutenant General Victor Afanasiev, the only military musician in the world who held the rank of General. The dancers with the band were joined by dancers from the world dance company based in Brisbane.

The Band of Her Majesty's Royal Marines Portsmouth returned with Marches from the Musicals before we embarked on another little bit of comedy as the Tattoo Choir wandered on to the arena dressed as though they had emerged from the audience and I urged them to return to their seats. Instead they formed up and sang more Songs from the Musicals.

The Omanis returned with the young Davidia Lind dancers dressed in vivid red as little devils leaping and squirming round the floor as the Omani drummers beat out a frenzied rhythm on their Middle Eastern drums. The Russian Army Central Band with three superb singers played a set of mainly Russian tunes and finished it with 'Waltzing Matilda', before the New Zealand Army Band marched on with another of its breathtaking sets, joined when it reached 'the Can Can' by the Davidia Lind dancers and acrobats who even outdid the energy of the Kiwis.

When all the bands had returned for the finale they began with 'The Dark Island', followed by 'The Gael' and the Grand March from *Aida* before they reached one of the most memorable performances I have ever heard of 'the 1812 Overture'. Piotr Tchaikovsky wrote the music to commemorate the Russian Army turning back Napoleon's forces from the gates of Moscow at the Battle of Borodina and I remain convinced that, as a Russian, General Afanasiev and the Russian Band drew something special and unexpected from Tchaikovsky's music, and out of the other bands, to create one of the most remarkable performances I have heard at tattoos around the world over many years.

1999 Sydney

The next year I was greatly flattered to be asked to come back to Australia to present the ANZAC Military Tattoo in Sydney's Entertainment Centre. Having spent seven years in Australia as a teenager I was aware of how sensitive the ANZAC memory is and how carefully I should tread and how thorough my research must be before I wrote a word of the script. To be quite sure I had a good start I went to the Imperial War Museum in London where the library staff could not have been more helpful. Even though this was an ANZAC Tattoo, it was still

The Great ANZAC Tattoo in Sydney.

strongly international with performers from the United Kingdom, Sweden, New Zealand, the United States of America and Trinidad and Tobago as well as Australia.

I wrote and read a brief description of the coming of age of the ANZACS at Gallipoli, which led into a reading of Lieutenant Colonel John McCrae's poem 'In Flanders Fields' by an actor in a First World War uniform, King Raymond, and then Moina Michael's 1918 response 'We Shall Keep the Faith' was read by a teenage girl, Melanie Wilson.

We rolled back the centuries with a presentation of the Ceremony of the Keys carried out nightly in the Tower of London. The keys are to the Tower what a Colour is to Regiment so they and the Yeoman Warder carrying them are carefully guarded every step of the way, in Sydney by the Queen's Colour Squadron of the Royal Air Force who guarded the Chief Yeoman Warder, Mr Hugh Thompson. It is a colourful piece of history which dates back 700 years and I did warn the audience that they must never call the Yeomen Warders Beefeaters

or they might be locked up in the Tower for the night.

The ceremony was followed by the Ceremonial Band of the Swedish Army playing a programme of Swedish music. Although I only had to introduce one of the pieces by name, it is a matter of pride that I make sure that I know how the names in a foreign tongue are properly pronounced. They were followed by the Band of the Coldstream Guards from Britain and then the Lochiel Marching Team from Wellington. Four local pipe bands were led by the Australian Juvenile Champion Drum Major, 17-year-old Douglas McFarland, and were joined by the Tattoo Highland Dancers and then the New Zealand Army Band which left the audience on a high for the interval.

I started the second half with a little comedy, saying that the lights felt they had not had the credit they deserved, and the lighting designer put on a clever show. Next, the Queen's Colour Squadron of the Royal Air Force put on a quite different show demonstrating their other role of providing close protection for RAF installations anywhere in the world. They gave way to the Bands of the Royal Australian Air Force and the Australian Army Band Sydney who played a completely Australian programme into which I had fun popping little prompts for the audience as the bands moved from one tune to another and the musicians joined in the fun playing Aussie Rules and rounding up sheep. By contrast the United States Air Force Honour Guard Drill Team was tightly drilled and dazzled the audience with its skill at drill before the Trinidad and Tobago Defence Force Steel Orchestra and Drums broke ranks and spread the sunshine of the Caribbean around the hall.

We paid our tribute to the Australian horsemen of the First World War with a superb reading of Banjo Paterson's 'The Man from Snowy River' by the Australian actor Hec McMillan and after the Evening Hymn and the Lone Piper I chose lines from Henry Lawson's poem 'The Men Who Made Australia' which seemed to catch the spirit of the last Tattoo I presented in the 20th century.

The sons of all
Australia, they were
born to conquer fate
And, where charity and
friendship are sincere,
Where a sinner is a brother
and stranger is a mate,
There the future of a
nation's written clear.

2000 Brisbane

After the fright of the collapsing stand in 1998 the Brisbane International Tattoo moved out to the Entertainment Centre at Boondall on the outskirts of the city. Although it was out of the city centre there was plenty of parking and space outside to rehearse in the sunshine.

Although Colin Harper was still the Artistic Producer, this Tattoo opened with the traditional Scottish sound of the pipes from ten pipe bands, followed by an Australian Aboriginal welcome by William Barton on the *yidarki* or didgeridoo which led into the Massed Bands of the Scots Guards, Pershing's Own from the United States, the Tongan Defence Force, the Australian Army Brisbane and the Royal Military College Duntroon. The United States Army Drill Team from the Third Infantry

– the Old Guard – based in Washington, DC, dazzled the audience with the skill of the their weapon handling. It was always a finely tuned challenge to time the narration of such an impeccable display so that it fitted the action and I enjoyed getting it right each time. In colourful contrast the Royal Corps of Musicians of the Tonga Defence Services and their Music Director Captain Ve'ehala returned with their Polynesian music, dancing warriors and, happily, the ladies with their elegant Tau'olunga dancing.

One of the advantages of working indoors is that you can use the roof to help and when the 9th Battalion of the Royal Queensland Regiment demonstrated some of their military skills they started by abseiling out of a 'helicopter', in reality from the roof, to see off a group of armed intruders. The Australian Army Bands were followed by a tug of war between the well-built musicians from Tonga and a group of local Naval Reserve Cadets. There were a lot more cadets than Tongans but they were well matched and each won a pull until on the third pull as I was urging the audience on to give the cadets greater encouragement a police dog joined the cadets' end of the rope and it was all over for the Tongans who let go their end of the rope.

That little bit of comedy gave way to Police Sergeant Glen Damro, dressed as a female, pushing a pram when he was attacked and robbed but the miscreant did not get far as Police Dog Titan leaped out of the pram, apprehended the offender and then jumped back into Sergeant Damro's arms. The audience rose to the pair when I revealed that it had been Sergeant Damro and Titan along with another officer who had captured the fruitpicker who, four months earlier, had set fire to a backpackers' hostel in Childers in Queensland, killing 15 people. Titan had been slashed by the killer as he brought the man down but as the audience could see had fully recovered and was perfectly capable of returning to work and raising a laugh with it. My younger son had been backpacking in Queensland at the time, fortunately not in Childers, so I had an anxious wait for confirmation that he had not been in that hostel.

After that start a team of six Queensland Police dogs and their handlers showed their skills at apprehending offenders and agility over some formidable obstacles and there was bit more comedy with Sergeant McJannett, dressed as a layabout, and his dog Jake challenging the police dogs to a race while I asked the audience if the police should accept the challenge, which of course they did.

The Band of the Scots Guards played us up to the interval and after it there was marvellous Scottish and Irish dancing and for the first time I saw a rival group of the marching girls from New Zealand, this time the Pioneers of Canterbury. The premier United States' Army Band Pershing's Own under their Leader and Commander, Colonel Gary Lamb, were led on by their Drum Major Sergeant Major James McGarity Junior wearing a bearskin headdress. He had spent years fighting the United States Army authorities to have it approved and eventually succeeded. Once the band had finished its set it was joined by the other bands in 'The Battle Hymn of the Republic'.

Like the Russians two years earlier, Colonel Lamb, as an American, seemed to draw something extra and special from this historic tune from the United States and the other bands and the Queensland Philharmonic Chorale and I have yet to hear a more moving performance of the music than I heard on that tattoo. As the bands played the last bar, members of the Queensland Defence Force Historical Association fired their muskets to put the seal on a memorable performance. Not even Ottorino Resphigi's mighty Pines of the Appian Way or Mercy Diez singing 'Amazing Grace' or Greg Moore's 'Will Ye No Come Back Again' could top the American tune that year.

Concerts in Melbourne and Brisbane

Sadly we did not come back for any more tattoos in Brisbane. I did return in 2001 for two concerts produced by Colin Harper but it was obvious that he was ill and sadly he died at the start of 2004. His concert in Melbourne, Scotland the Brave, was a celebration of Scottish music. I wrote an article for the Melbourne programme about the enduring appeal of Scottish music and finished it by saying that 'it is because it touches everyday life and it touches the heart. It has a simple direct appeal which remains distinctive and different and as long as there are people whose hearts can be touched Scottish music will endure.' I even recited Robert Burns' 'Address to a Haggis'. The Brisbane concert *The Celts Are Coming* had many of the same performers but broadened the music to include Welsh and Irish and even Cornish as well as Scottish songs and tunes. The Scottish dancers even did a quite startling and memorable Can Can.

Bermuda

Between the two concerts I had been asked by the Imps to commentate for their motor cycle display in Bermuda. They had been asked to show their daring skills at the 64th Agricultural Exhibition in Bermuda. Bermuda is one of those faraway places one hears about but never finds time to visit so I jumped at the chance. We flew through Toronto and were greeted

at Bermuda Airport by the Town Crier Michael Jones. As well as the show there were radio interviews and visits, including a reception by the Mayor at the City Hall where we did a mini-tattoo the following week and we were even received at Government House by the Governor, His Excellency Thorold Masefield CMG, before we went to the Agricultural Exhibition where I narrated a total of seven shows over three days

Bermuda was a fascinating place. It had been the inspiration for William Shakespeare's *The Tempest* and I had not realised that it had no running water. Every drop has to be collected from the sky or by the desalination of seawater. The attractively painted houses gather their water in cisterns. To establish a settlement on Bermuda must have needed a great deal of faith and ingenuity. Nor had I realised that the island only allowed households one motor vehicle and, when we went, motor cycles were restricted to 100cc so the locals were envious of the youngsters riding 250cc bikes. The ground was rock hard but the shows were a great success. Having time to get to know the young riders and who was doing what helped enormously to put the right name to the right rider hidden under their big crash helmets. After the show I was presented with a handsome crest of Bermuda which sits on my wall as a happy reminder of the show and when we came home I wrote and narrated a video of the visit.

While I was there I saw the Gombey Dancers and the Bermuda Regiment, recommended them to the Producer in Edinburgh and both arrived two years later. But I also caught something nasty and set off to narrate the concert in Brisbane feeling rotten. When I stepped off the plane in Brisbane I was met by my best friend from Brisbane State High School, Desmond Milliner, who was a doctor further up the coast. He and his wife Pam took me home, dosed me with antibiotics and put me to bed. Later Des told me he was not sure if I would make it through the night but thanks to his medical skills and attention I did and have stayed for a few more years beyond.

2006 Sydney

I did not return to Australia again until we took the Edinburgh Tattoo there in 2005 and the following year I was back again to co-narrate an ANZAC International Military Tattoo at the Sydney Superdome. This show was produced by Kerry Jewel, whose father was the British comedian Jimmy Jewel best known for his partnership with Ben Warriss. Kerry had asked his old friend Barry Eaton, a well-known radio and television presenter, to narrate the show with me, I assumed, to gain experience to present future shows. This show was held indoors which allowed full control of light

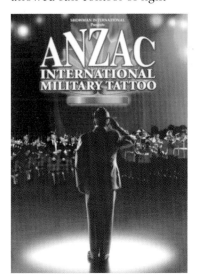

The ANZAC International Tattoo in Sydney.

and sound so we were able to begin in darkness with a film from the First World War and two horsemen carrying the Australian and New Zealand flags circling the arena before the National Anthems of Australia and New Zealand and the start of the show. The Lochiel Marching Drill Team from Wellington accompanied by the New Zealand Army Band gave their immaculate display of entertaining marching to music before the Band of Her Majesty's Royal Marines Portsmouth played a set of nautical tunes as a reminder of the role of the navies during the Great War

The Thula Sizwe Zulu dancers from South Africa showed us the rituals which Zulu warriors went through to chase away evil spirits before the warriors from Tonga brought us the sound of a fangu fangu as they attacked in war canoes, the kailao war dance and finally the graceful *tau'olunga* hand dancing of the ladies and the massed pipes drums took us to the interval. The New Zealand Army Band raced through another breathtaking performance before the Band of the Grenadier Guards,

celebrating the Regiment's 350th anniversary, steadied the show marching and playing as only the Guards can. The New South Wales Millennium Band of young student musicians playing wartime tunes led into a display of rescue techniques by the New South Wales Police Rescue and Bomb Disposal Unit, followed by Highland dancing by the OzScot dancers who were regular dancers at Edinburgh together with the Sydney Irish Dance Ensemble.

We honoured the ANZACS with the Marines Band playing Demir Demirkan's Gelibolu written for a Turkish film about Gallipoli and sung by 12-year-old boy soprano Dion Condack. Then we welcomed six ANZAC Veterans as I read the words the Turkish commander Mustafa Kemal Atatürk wrote on the Gallipoli memorial 'You, the mothers, who sent your sons from far away countries, wipe away your tears; your sons are now lying in our bosom and are in peace. After having lost their lives on this land they have become our sons as well.' The Australian actor Bill Kerr, well remembered for his appearances in many British films and in the radio comedy *Hancock's Half Hour*, read Laurence Binyon's poem 'For the Fallen' and after a minute's silence, and piper Lincoln Hilton playing 'The Flowers of the Forest', the tenor Benjamin Makisi sang 'You Raise Me Up'.

The show had been timed to coincide with ANZAC Day so on the morning of 25 April I pinned on my medals, donned my red beret and stepped out on the ANZAC Day Parade in Sydney. It was a long parade with a good deal of hanging about but I marched proudly in a unique procession.

I heard later that the Tattoo had not been a financial success but the following year, another similar event in Australia was planned by the same team under the title of *A Salute to Heroes*. I noticed in the prospectus that Barry was listed as the only narrator of the 2006 show so I did not expect to be asked back and learned the 2007 show had been abandoned after making a start in Perth. The *Sydney Morning Herald* reported that the show's investors had gone to court to freeze the box office takings from the first show and the organisers could not pay the bills. It was

a great shame and I heard that at least one British band had to find its own way home.

Moscow

In 2007 I had been asked if I would be available to go to Moscow for a new tattoo run by Vitaly Mironov, who had taken part in the 'peace treaty' ceremony with Berwick in 2001. I was never quite sure what my role was to be but attempting to repair a tile on my roof I fell off and spent some time in hospital recovering from concussion and broken ribs. Although the producer kept asking if I would be able to go, I eventually had to say I would not recover in time and had to abandon the trip and the expensive visa I had gone to such trouble to obtain.

Ipswich, Queensland

Late in 2007, I was well on the way to recovery when I was approached by Joe McGhee, an enthusiastic piper originally from Glasgow but now living in Ipswich not far from Brisbane in Queensland, to ask if I would narrate a little tattoo in Ipswich the following year. I readily agreed and on 11 April 2008 set off to fly from

Edinburgh through London
Heathrow and on to Singapore
and Melbourne arriving in
Brisbane two days later. It was
shortly after the new Terminal
Five at Heathrow had opened
and I was intrigued to see it
but grew apprehensive when
I reached Melbourne and my
case with all my kilt equipment
did not. I reported it and
flew on to Brisbane without
the case. I rang regularly to
check if it had been reported
anywhere. Joe was worried
because he had booked me to
speak at the Ipswich Rotary
Club two days later and he
was keen that I should appear
in a kilt and black tie. It hardly
seems likely but between
Ipswich and Brisbane there

is a kilt making and hiring
business, so we went straight
there and found a Henderson
tartan kilt which the owner
agreed to make fit by the next
day and we hired all the rest
of those things necessary to
equip a Scot to speak at an
Australian Rotary Club dinner.
The next day my case turned
up, it had gone to Los Angeles
while I had gone to Brisbane.
I knew that Terminal Five had
been having a lot of difficulty
directing luggage to the places
it was intended to go but all
ended well and I was able to
return the hired outfit and
wear my own clothes again.

This was the fifth Ipswich
International Tattoo and was
titled *A Celtic Journey*. It
was a stage show badged as a
tattoo held in the Ipswich Civic
Hall. The usual narrator – a
very nice chap called Warrick
Jackes, a civilian employee
with the Queensland Police
Service and a goalball judge
– seemed happy to sit this
one out but I thought that
if we worked together he
would learn something about
tattoo presentation for the
future. Joe was a piper with
Ipswich Thistle Pipe Band and
he had drawn in two other
bands to make a full sound

in the theatre. There was Irish dancing and Highland dancing and Gaelic singing from a family dance troupe of four brothers and two sisters known as Gaelic Dream, the Small Pipes Society brought a different piping sound and the Viva La Musica Orchestra changed the mood before the Queensland Irish Pipe Band played some rollicking Irish tunes and the award winning Cambrian Choir from South East Queensland took us to the interval. The Ipswich Returned and Services League Youth Band opened up the second half, followed by a Celtic folk group, Murphy's Pigs, more Highland dancing and piping and the Royal Australian Air Force cadets based at nearby RAAF Amberley gave an impressive display of precision drill. The lovely singer Kathleen Proctor-Moore, who started her career in the Scottish city of Perth, sang 'Danny Boy' and 'When the Pipers Play' before the whole cast returned for 'Amazing Grace'. It was an adventurous little show and I was proud to have been able to play a part in it.

Like the Tattoo in Sydney in 2006 it had been timed to coincide with ANZAC Day and I was honoured to be asked by the Senior Vice President of the Returned and Services League in Ipswich, Keith Fraser, to attend a dawn service at half past four and to be the Special Guest and Speaker at the Wreath Laying Service at the Nicholas Street Memorial Gardens in Ipswich where I reminded the audience that Scottish Borderers had fought and died alongside the ANZACs at Gallipoli. Later I had the honour of carrying the Union Jack in the march to the larger service for the public at 11 o'clock.

When I was still a teenager in Melbourne I joined the athletics club for which the great Australian runner Ron Clarke competed. He set 17 world records in his illustrious career. As it happened, at the same time that I was the Convener of Scottish Borders Council, Ron was the Mayor of Queensland's Gold Coast Council and when the Tattoo had finished I drove down to Southport where the Council offices were situated and had tea with Ron in the Mayor's parlour. We caught up on the many intervening years and he told me that the coldest place he had ever run was at the Commonwealth Games at Meadowbank in Edinburgh in 1970 when he took the 10,000 metres silver medal behind Scotland's Lachie Stewart. The meeting was one of those happy chances to peel away the years and I will always be grateful to Joe McGhee for making it possible. But that was not all I had to thank Joe for. He held a farewell barbecue at his home and during the course of a really happy evening among friends he presented me with the Henderson kilt which had been so swiftly tailored to fit me for the Rotary dinner two weeks earlier. My old kilt had 'shrunk' so this was a marvellous gift which I treasure still.

Concerts in Toronto and New York
The following year I had a most intriguing request to narrate two more *Scotland the Brave* concerts in Toronto and New York. They were being arranged by Andrew McKinnon, the same promoter who had arranged the Melbourne concert in 2001. We played two concerts in early April, one in the Roy Thomson Hall in Toronto, the other six days later in the Avery Fisher Hall at the Lincoln Centre on New York's Broadway timed to get us close to Tartan Day. Andrew and his Director of Music Sean O'Boyle picked up session musicians for the orchestras and local choirs and dancers in both cities and took with them the soprano Suellan Cusack, the tenor Greg Moore, Pipe Major Andrew Fuller, fiddler Marcus Holden and pianist Catherine Lynagh. The music was almost completely Scottish, with a couple of Irish tunes thrown in, although the principal performers were all Australian. The show was superb and i was flabbergasted towards the end of the concert in new york as i walked on stage to announce 'Auld Lang Syne' when i realised that the audience was on its collective feet giving the show a standing ovation – on Broadway. I wondered for only a moment whether to ask them to sit down again because we had not quite finished but decided that the cast should enjoy the moment which seemed to last for a long time before we could play to the end when the audience repeated

its rapturous appreciation of what had been a superb show which thoroughly deserved its reception.

Voorthuizen

In 2010 I was asked by George Alblas, a teacher from the Dutch town of Voorthuizen, if I would come and narrate a special Tattoo being held in May as part of the National celebrations organised by the Thank You Canada and Allied Forces Committee to honour the Veterans, mainly Canadians, who had liberated the Netherlands from its Nazi occupiers in 1945. The Tattoo would be held in the outdoor Roelenengweg Stadium in Voortheuizen. George Alblas was a regular visitor to the Edinburgh Tattoo and had marched on it as a Drum Major and would be the Drum Major on this Tattoo.

George had attracted from Canada the Lincoln and Welland Band, from the United Kingdom The Royal Edinburgh Military Tattoo Highland dancers, the band of the Welsh Guards, the band of Her Majesty's Royal Marines Scotland and six pipe bands plus two others from Oman and the Netherlands, from France the Musique Equipage de la Flotte de Brest, from Poland the representative Orchestra of the Pomeranian District, from the Caribbean the Trinidad and Tobago Defence Force Steel Orchestra and Drums and from the Netherlands the Fanfare Corps of the Netherlands Reserve. There were also the performers of the Gordon Highlanders re-enactment group and the Guard of Honour provided by the volunteers of the Hussars of Venlo. It was a good little Tattoo playing to smaller crowds than it deserved. It was also interesting to see the celebration parade in Apeldoorn and how many people crowded into the streets to greet the Canadian veterans 65 years after the liberation. George very kindly drove me over to Arnhem where the British and Polish airborne forces had fought their most famous battle of the Second World War and showed me the dropping zone, the Hartenstein Hotel which had been the airborne headquarters and is now the Airborne Museum and the Airborne Cemetery near Oosterbeek where so many of the men who jumped into the Netherlands on Operation Market Garden still lie.

Las Vegas

The following spring I was invited to narrate an International Military Tattoo in Las Vegas, Nevada. It was being produced by Major Bruce Hitchings, who was to go on to produce the Highland Tattoos at Fort George, and was under the overall control of a retired Nevada State Senator, Dennis Nolan. The show would not be held on the famous Las Vegas Strip but at the fine Thomas & Mack Centre's indoor arena. I thought we had made it when, walking along the Strip, I noticed a big sign advertising TATTOO – but it was for the other kind. I was staying in the accommodation attached to Terribles Casino and had to negotiate rows and rows of gaming machines and tables to get from the front door to the rooms at the back. I suppose they were designed to be tempting but I did not succumb.

The show had drawn the pipes and drums of the First Battalion Scots Guards, and from North America the Pipes and Drums of the Canadian Forces, Vancouver Police Pipe Band and Winnipeg Police Pipe Band under the Senior Drum Major in the British Army Drum Major Brian Alexander of the Royal Regiment of Scotland and Senior Pipe Major Robert Watt. The United States Marine Corps Air Ground Combat Centre Band from Twentynine Palms, California, with Master Sergeant Eric Howells narrating, told the story of the American National Anthem. Canada's pre-eminent military musical ensemble, the Canadian Forces Band, a highly versatile group embracing the historic Pipes and Drums and the contemporary Show Band, featured a Las Vegas medley.

The para-rescue men from nearby Nellis Air Force Base carried out a reenactment of a dramatic rescue of a downed pilot. The United States Navy Band Southwest, a particularly important part of San Diego's military heritage, played 'Songs of Sailor and Sea' before they broke into Elvis Presley numbers more likely to be familiar in Las Vegas. Then Highland Dancers drawn from serving soldiers in the First Battalion Scots

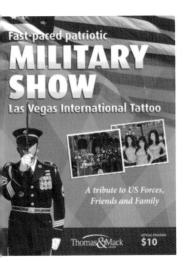

Sharon Lynn's Celtic Crown and Caravan gave the crowd a fine display of Irish dancing.

I had some nice tattoo banter with an Elvis impersonator who we had arranged would appear during my description of the origin of tattoos, interrupt me and sing 'A Little Less Conversation, A Little More Action Please' and later 'Wooden Heart'. It made a happy link for me because my elder son and his wife had been married in Las Vegas in the Graceland Chapel by an Elvis impersonator but not the same one. Tom and his wife flew down from their home in Indiana with their little daughter Aline and hired a car so they were able to drive me to the chapel and further out around the famous Nevada town. I had booked them a room in the casino but that booking disappeared so I moved them into my 'suite' and bunked down on the couch which was quite comfortable enough. It was lovely to see them all and have a chance to spend time with them. Tom put a coin in one of the slot machines as he was passing and got a handsome-sounding payout. After the show was all over and they had

Guards, recently back from Afghanistan, performed the sword dance and then an international team of ladies from Scotland, the United States and Canada showed us how Argyll Broadswords should be danced. The Old Guard, the United States Army Drill Team thrilled the audience with a nine-minute display of skill in weapon handling. I had narrated their display in the past and it was a pleasure to be able to do it with them again on their own side of the Atlantic before the United States Air Force Band of the Golden West recreated the unmistakable Glenn Miller sound with a well chosen medley. The Wicked Tinkers played up a Gaelic storm and flown back, former Senator Nolan slipped a cheque under my door in payment but 'forgot' to sign it so he got the script and the narration free. I hope he slept well. Major Hitchings very kindly reimbursed my air fare. I guess Las Vegas was bound to be a gamble but although I lost the fee I won the experience of working with a number of new people I had not met before.

Paderborn

In 2013 a sharp-eyed Army officer in Germany had spotted my name on a social media site and asked if I would be prepared to come to Paderborn in Germany and narrate a small tattoo which was being billed as a Military Musical Extravaganza. It was to help sugar the pill of the British withdrawal from the town in 2017 and having been on exercises many times in the Paderborn area I was happy to help. I was especially delighted to introduce at last the Band of my own Regiment, the Parachute Regiment, who began with a piece of music Royal Occasion composed by their Director of Music, Captain Evin Frost, to celebrate the birth of Prince

George in July. There were the Pipes and Drums of the Royal Dragoon Guards and the Queens Royal Hussars both wearing the saffron kilt. The Bugles of 5 Rifles moved at their fast Light Infantry pace. The Paderborn/Gutersloh Military Wives Choir took us to a little interval during which the arena was set up for a well-run display by 102 Military Working Dog Squadron of the First Military Working Dog Regiment. The Heeresmusickorps from Hanover represented the host nation. The Llanelli Male Voice Choir gave us a wonderful sound of Wales and the bands played 'Highland Cathedral' and then John Miles' 'Music' before the traditional ending.

It was an unusual show in that I was sharing the commentary with a German speaker, Kai Huttrop-Hage, who I had not met before the show. Kai was an amiable German whose principal announcing was at horse shows but he fitted in superbly and I enjoyed working with him. The show was held on the Schutzenplatz horse-jumping arena which had a large tree in the centre around which the acts had to pivot. Kai and I had been plonked in an Army tent which gave us a partial view of the arena. We each had a microphone and no light by which to read our scripts. So although the weather had been wet we picked up the table and our two chairs, carried them to the rail around the ring and made the arrangement work. The same phenomenon seems to be common in many places. The idea that the narrator of whatever it may be could need a light always seems to surprise the sound providers. I always carry a small torch just in case.

The Paderborn Garrison decided to give the show a second outing the following year. The Bugles of 3 and 5 Rifles, the Band of the Brigade of Gurkhas, the Pipes and Drums of the Royal Scots Borderers First Battalion Royal Regiment of Scotland and the British Forces Germany Military Wives Choir filled the first half. Then the Princess of Wales Royal Regiment laid on a rather entertaining display of how physical training had evolved with combat conditioning, a log to build up strength and then a 'gun run' to give a little edge to the training. The Heeresmusickorps from Kassel, the Crossed Swords Pipes and Drums and the elite ceremonial Drill Team from the Seventh Company of the German Guard Battalion represented the host country. I was glad to work with Kai Huttrop-Hage again, we made a good team.

Getting home became nerve-wracking early the next morning when the Army driver I had expected outside the barracks had not turned up half an hour after the appointed time. I dug out the splendidly efficient and obliging Garrison Support Officer who detailed another driver who drove swiftly and safely to Dusseldorf in time to catch the flight to Newcastle. As the officer who had organised the shows was to be posted back to the UK, I suspected that this would be the last Paderborn Tattoo and so it proved to be.

New York

Earlier in the year I had been approached to write and present a tattoo in New York which would coincide with Tartan Day there. The Mason Hall theatre in the

The programme for the New York Tattoo, 2014.

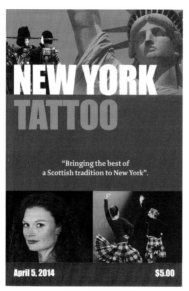

NEW YORK TATTOO

"Bringing the best of a Scottish tradition to New York".

April 5, 2014 $5.00

Baruch College Performing Arts Center on Lexington Avenue would be the home of this show which, I was told, would be the first tattoo in the city for 50 years. Major Bruce Hitchings, who had produced the show in Las Vegas three years earlier, was the producer of the event which had drawn most of its cast from around New York. As so often happens, rehearsals were limited but somehow we were more or less ready by the evening of Tartan Day and the West Point Hellcats sent us off with a fanfare and the American National Anthem sung by Scottish-born soprano Lesley Craigie which was followed by the combined sound of the New York Metro Pipe Band, Cockenzie & Port Seton, Royal British Legion Scotland and Forfar and District Pipes and Drums from Scotland and from Canada the Sons of Scotland under the control of a guest drum major from Las Vegas Ken Misch. The Hellcats brought us their splendid presentation on the hardships and the joys of serving their country in the military and Irish dancers were accompanied by an Irish-American group, Jameson's Revenge.

I had to comprehend and then present the ceremony of the passing over of a shepherd's crook of office from one National Trust for Scotland Clan Ambassador to the next. For a year the stick had been with the first ambassadors the Clan McPherson and was passing to the Clan Hamilton. The Clan Ambassador programme was established to honour the Clans of Highland Scotland and help raise awareness and finance in America to conserve some of Scotland's finest natural and built heritage. This little ceremony was only mentioned in passing before the Tattoo so it needed some swift research and preparation to ensure that the exchange passed off smoothly.

Haley Hewitt from Hartford, Connecticut the National Scottish Harp Champion of America graced the tattoo with a couple of tunes before Lesley Craigie joined her to sing the 'Eriskay Love Lilt'. The New York Metro Pipe Band played an original and entertaining set with World Champion Drum Major Jason Paguio demonstrating his skills with the mace before their Drum Corps took centre stage. The Patriot Brass group from New Jersey, which exists to provide affordable music for military veterans, played first Semper Fidelis and then an Armed Forces Medley for which I asked 'If you are serving or you are a veteran we ask you to stand, if you are able, and be recognised for your service to your country. We also invite your family members to stand in solidarity.' Many did.

The group of International Highland Dancers led by former World Champion Rachel McLagan gave an upbeat display of a march, strathspeys and reels before the playing and singing of 'The Green Fields of France', 'Wooden Heart' and 'Amazing Grace'. The United States Coastguard Honor Guard marched on for 'Auld Lang Syne', 'How Great Thou Art' and the Last Post. It had been a scramble but in the end the show gave the audience a taste of an entertainment which has become a Scottish international success story.

The Silver Year

I HAVE BEEN lucky enough to be presenting tattoos for the last 25 years and in that time it has been obvious that the tattoo formula remains enduringly popular in countries around the world. I have been lucky enough to narrate some of them but I see advertisements for many more, some of which seem to be repeated year after year, others pop up once or twice and then fizzle out. A tattoo looks straightforward but making it happen is a lot harder than it looks.

I heard of one tattoo staged in a city which had a large service presence that should have guaranteed a big audience. But it sounded as though the organisers had merely transferred a stage show with two comperes into a large arena. It lasted for two seasons and folded I think because the planning had failed to grasp that in the 21st century a tattoo has to be spectacular and swift-moving with a lot of colour and music. Two tiny figures in a big arena cracking jokes to each other which are hard to hear will not and did not thrill the audience – many of whom, I was told, walked out during the performance.

A tattoo is like a swan or even an iceberg. Like a swan, it should glide serenely through each performance, while a lot of hard work is going on out of sight to make it look easy. Like an iceberg, only the performers should be visible to the public but there is always a great deal more of the preparation and support which the audience does not see.

I am always surprised when people tell me that they saw the Edinburgh Tattoo many years ago and do not need to see it again. They think it is the same old show every year and have not grasped that the Tattoo is always evolving and every year is different. In the

25 years I have been writing and presenting 'the greatest show on earth' I have seen it change. The Tattoo in the second decade of the 21st century is quite different to the shows of its first 40 years. Its pace has become faster – the acts almost tumble over each other and it is certainly not a display of marching bands, although old videos show that it was never that.

The script and the narration are only one part of the complex jigsaw but a terribly obvious part if they go wrong. Even when they do not, there is a small group of correspondents who will seek out a tiny molehill from which they like to build a mountain. Usually they have half-heard something, which it turns out was not what I had said. I do my best to take care to be historically accurate and aware of people's sensitivities when I am writing the script and addressing the audience, but even performers can forget that the Tattoo is an entertainment to thrill the public and not a historical seminar.

I always write a very full script with all that I am going to say and also all the stage directions and extra pieces of detail as well so that if anything were to happen to me someone else should be able to pick up the script and carry on. I am proud to say that I have not missed a single performance in 25 years so that has never been put to the test.

As with any live event there will be moments which cannot be predicted and the narrator needs to think quickly and be ready to cope. One night someone fell ill in the stands moments before the show began and, although only the people round about knew that something was wrong, we could not start until the first aid team and ambulance crew had assessed the patient and decided what was best for him. I had to keep the audience's attention that night and have done it on other nights for other reasons when there has been a delay. I carry detailed background notes on the history of the Castle, on the One O'Clock Gun and on the monuments around the Esplanade under the stands. When I first enquired about the monuments I found that no-one had previously prepared a description of them so I spent some time noting what was there and researching each one.

Although the Tattoo has never been cancelled because of the weather, some conditions – high winds, heavy rain and sea mist – can have an effect. Drill teams throwing rifles with bayonets over their shoulders behind them in a high wind is dangerous. Even handling the rifles when they are wet can be tricky and gymnasts cannot use some of their equipment when it is wet, although motorcycle display teams cope with the rain remarkably well. It is rare but occasionally the North Sea *haar* or sea mist is so thick that it makes the fireworks on the Castle difficult or impossible to see but in 25 years we have only cancelled the fireworks once because of that. We have cancelled or stopped the fireworks when a high wind was in danger of, or was, blowing burning sparks into the audience. We always have a fire engine on standby in the Castle and occasionally the crew has had to extinguish fires in the foliage within the Castle or on the Castle rock.

Failures of the equipment which controls the power, the lights and the sound are exceedingly rare – although one night the power went down and so did my microphone. For a little while I was unable to carry on with the narration and was reduced to shouting out of the window to the Drum Major at the front of the pipes and drums, 'Carry on, Drum Major.' I am not sure whether he heard me or not but he did carry on.

It is remarkable that nowadays we can gather together our performers from around the world on a Sunday night and after three days of intense rehearsals have a show ready for the public on the fourth day. People often ask how we manage to weld such a diverse cast into such a magnificent show year after year. I think it is because they come well prepared and the rehearsals to knit the show together are intense.

They start on a Monday morning early and during the day each item rehearses individually at Redford Barracks and in the evening on the Castle Esplanade until 11.00 pm on the first two days. By the Wednesday morning we are ready to put the elements together into a continuous show at Redford Barracks

Alasdair Hutton collects messages from pipers and drummers before the show.

and invite local residents and disabled groups to come and see it. Their response is a good guide to how the audiences up at the Castle are likely to react.

Getting the cast up to the Castle each night is a great spectacle in itself. They are taken in buses on to the Castle Esplanade, where I am always astonished at how many buses can be shoehorned on to the relatively small area before the performers all disembark and head for the rest areas where they can relax and change and prepare for their performances.

What I always find remarkable is the huge range of countries which are represented in the audience.

I am still a little surprised at how much people enjoy hearing themselves and their countries mentioned in my warm-up. There are always the old Commonwealth countries – Australia, Canada, New Zealand and South Africa plus of course America – but nowadays there are big contingents from places as diverse as Korea and Switzerland and these seem to change slowly year by year.

In days past the performers used to play the fool on the very last performance each year, wearing odd hats or exchanging bits of uniform or rolling oranges down the Esplanade in the dark. It was fun for the performers to let their hair down but incomprehensible to the audiences who had paid to see the same show as everyone else. With regret, we have to ask the cast each year to play the same show every night right through to the end.

I am interested to note two things which are just the same in Edinburgh as they were away back before the Second World War in Aldershot. In both places Scouts help sell the programmes and, as in Aldershot, the Tattoo in Edinburgh raises huge amounts of money for military charities. We have donated some £8 million since 1950 to the charities of all three services and to arts organisations. We now give work experience to young men with criminal records on the Tattoo Support Group, which helps move equipment on and off the Esplanade during the shows.

We have been fortunate to have had support from the General Officers Commanding the Army in Scotland who had quickly grasped the value of the shop window on the services which the Tattoo provided to the live audiences and the bigger television audiences and were largely sympathetic to our request for military support.

Over the years I have had enormous pleasure in presenting many other tattoos in other countries and around the United Kingdom, as well as hundreds of concerts mainly to raise money for service charities, other parades and Beating Retreat ceremonies, including the Household Division's magnificent annual performance on Horseguards Parade each June just before Trooping the Colour, and many events for Armed Forces Day nationally and locally. It has been a great pleasure and a great honour to work with many distinguished Directors of Music, some of whom have become friends, and many bands which pop up at different events in different countries. I think that having a military background has made it so much easier to work with people who know that I understand the military culture.

Each of the tattoos has been similar but different, and each has been entertaining, and they have all given me the chance to directly compare what we do in Edinburgh with what other producers in other countries and other towns have done. So I can say with confidence that all have tried and some have come near but none has been able to match the quality and the flair of Edinburgh.

Because we have been doing the show in Edinburgh for almost 70 years we are happy to share our expertise with other tattoo producers around the world who come to Edinburgh to see how we do it. We are proud of the standard we have built up and are happy to help raise the standard of all the other shows which aspire to copy Edinburgh.

As I sit up in the storyteller's box looking out at the huge audiences I often wonder why people beat a path to Scotland from all over the world to sit in the open air in what we humorously call the summer.

I think there are three reasons.

The first is the setting, which is unrivalled with the backdrop of the old castle. On a fine summer's night, of which we get more than you might think, it is magnificent, towering into the night sky. It must have a certain appeal when so many similar shows try to replicate a castle as a backdrop.

The second is the sight and sound of the Massed Pipes and Drums. The spectacle of a couple of hundred pipers and drummers spilling over the draw bridge out of the Castle always brings prolonged applause from the big audiences every night.

Third is the international spectacle. Audiences can see at the Tattoo in Edinburgh a huge variety of performers from all over the world, from Chinese drummers to steel bands from the Caribbean, marching girls from New Zealand to frenetic Zulu drummers, from traditional dancers from the Indian hills or the South Pacific islands to big bands from the United States of America.

In Scotland we can often be our own worst enemies and seem to enjoy belittling anyone who seems to be succeeding; we have a terribly dismissive phrase 'I kent his faither' – in other words, there's nothing special about him so he had better not get above himself (or herself, for that matter).

But The Royal Edinburgh Military Tattoo is one of the great Scottish success stories.

Breathes there the man
with soul so dead
Who never to himself
hath said
This is my own, my
native land.
Land of brown heath
and shaggy wood
Land of the mountain
and the flood
Land of my sires.
What mortal hand could
ere untie the filial band
That knits me to thy
rugged strand?

We have been exporting the
show on television for more
than 50 years to more than
100 million people around
the world every year and
once Indian and Chinese
viewers fully join these audiences they will zoom to
around the billion mark.

In this show we can all be
proud that in Scotland The
Royal Edinburgh Military
Tattoo team has shown
that our traditions and
our skills *are* world-class.
They have produced and
will go on producing the
'greatest show on Earth'.

It would only be right to
finish this glance back over
25 years as I finish each
Royal Edinburgh Military
Tattoo, with the ringing
words of Sir Walter Scott:

THE GREATEST SHOW ON EARTH

Also published by **LUATH PRESS**

The Tattoo Fox
Alasdair Hutton
Illustrated by Stref
ISBN 9781908373939 PBK £5.99

A little fox makes her home by Edinburgh Castle and with the help of her new friend, the Castle Cat, she settles in well.

But there is one question the Castle Cat refuses to answer. What is the Tattoo?
'Just wait and see,' he tells her.
Will she ever find out?

This heart-warming tale was inspired by a real-life encounter between the Producer of the Royal Edinburgh Military Tattoo and a fox, late one night on the Castle Esplanade.

The Tattoo Fox Makes New Friends
Alasdair Hutton
Illustrated by Stref
ISBN 9781910021477 PBK £5.99

The fox's friends all gather round
To watch the greatest show in town

After discovering Edinburgh's Military Tattoo and setting up her home by Edinburgh Castle, the Tattoo Fox returns to her adventures around Edinburgh.

Meeting and making lots of new friends along the way (including the Queen!), the Tattoo Fox invites them all to her party.

Hutton is one of Scotland's greatest storytellers [and] the illustrations by Stref are the icing on the cake.
BRIGADIER DAVID ALLFREY MBE

Lots of adventures [and] the famous Tattoo creates a dramatic finale to the story.
JENNY BLANCH, *Carousel*

A hit with young readers. EDINBURGH EVENING NEWS

Details of these and other books published by Luath Press can be found at:
www.luath.co.uk

Luath Press Limited

committed to publishing well written books worth reading

LUATH PRESS takes its name from Robert Burns, whose little collie Luath (*Gael.*, swift or nimble) tripped up Jean Armour at a wedding and gave him the chance to speak to the woman who was to be his wife and the abiding love of his life. Burns called one of the 'Twa Dogs' Luath after Cuchullin's hunting dog in Ossian's *Fingal*. Luath Press was established in 1981 in the heart of Burns country, and is now based a few steps up the road from Burns' first lodgings on Edinburgh's Royal Mile. Luath offers you distinctive writing with a hint of unexpected pleasures.

Most bookshops in the UK, the US, Canada, Australia, New Zealand and parts of Europe, either carry our books in stock or can order them for you. To order direct from us, please send a £sterling cheque, postal order, international money order or your credit card details (number, address of cardholder and expiry date) to us at the address below. Please add post and packing as follows: UK – £1.00 per delivery address; overseas surface mail – £2.50 per delivery address; overseas airmail – £3.50 for the first book to each delivery address, plus £1.00 for each additional book by airmail to the same address. If your order is a gift, we will happily enclose your card or message at no extra charge.

Luath Press Limited
543/2 Castlehill
The Royal Mile
Edinburgh EH1 2ND
Scotland
Telephone: +44 (0)131 225 4326 (24 hours)
email: sales@luath. co.uk
Website: www.luath.co.uk